MYSTERIOUS
GLOUCESTERSHIRE

MYSTERIOUS
GLOUCESTERSHIRE

MARK TURNER

The
History
Press

Frontispiece: *Devil Figure at Winchcombe Church.*

First published 2011

The History Press
The Mill, Brimscombe Port
Stroud, Gloucestershire, GL5 2QG
www.thehistorypress.co.uk

ISBN 978 0 7524 5425 2

Typesetting and origination by The History Press
Printed in Great Britain

CONTENTS

ABOUT THE AUTHOR

Raised in the Welsh border town of Monmouth, the author spent countless childhood hours exploring the Forest of Dean around Staunton and Coleford, going on to develop a keen interest in history and folklore. He subsequently served for four years as a soldier in 1st The Queen's Dragoon Guards and then, in 1979, became a policeman with the Gloucestershire Constabulary. Much of his subsequent twenty-two years' police service was spent in the North Cotswolds, where his extensive knowledge of folklore and local history led to the publication of several books on the area. On retiring from the police in 2001 he commenced a career in the voluntary sector, while continuing to pursue an interest in the quirky side of the county's history.

INTRODUCTION

What characteristics make a place or event 'mysterious'? A glance through almost any dictionary or thesaurus reveals that the word is generally used to describe something puzzling, strange, secret or inexplicable. In our modern age of technology and almost limitless exploration, is there anything left that can be called truly mysterious? The accounts described in this book suggest that – in Gloucestershire, at least – there is much that is cloaked in mystery and superstition and, although some stories are based on little more than folklore, others offer much food for thought and discussion.

Ghosts and apparitions quite definitely fall into the 'mysterious' category, with many stories and personal accounts containing strange and inexplicable aspects. Claimed sightings of unidentified flying objects are invariably puzzling and, though sceptics may refute this, often cannot be easily explained. In relatively recent years, too, reported sightings of 'alien big cats' such as black panthers have added to the ever-growing list of mysterious occurrences in the British countryside. If one looks back through history, however, it can be seen that such mysteries are hardly a modern phenomenon. There are various legends of dragons and serpents and many churches, for example, are adorned with images of alien creatures and monsters, as well as ancient and pagan symbols such as the enigmatic 'green man'.

It may disappoint some readers to find a complete absence of 'crop circles'. This is because most of the elaborate and puzzling designs that have appeared in this part of the UK have been in Oxfordshire and, to a greater extent, Wiltshire. Very few have appeared in Gloucestershire, and in any case these complex art forms are widely regarded as the work of human hands.

Mysterious Gloucestershire does not seek to provide solutions to the centuries-old puzzle of ghosts and other apparently inexplicable phenomena. Over the years, various publications have sought to address the subject and, rather than concentrating on theories and 'explanations', this book simply seeks to offer the reader a useful and unusual guide to the county. The clear and precise gazetteer format is intended to provide a summary of all that is inexplicable and 'mysterious' about each town or village.

Some readers may feel they detect a degree of scepticism in the tone of my writing. I readily confess to suspecting that some of the accounts passed to me have rather more to do with fantasy than with the paranormal. I do not feel qualified to dismiss any of these stories, however, preferring instead to consider them as examples of living folklore. In many cases, though, accounts were given by people of a very balanced, cautious temperament whose experiences cannot easily be explained. It seems to me that in such cases there really are grounds for believing some of the events, in this book, to be genuinely mysterious.

The stories and accounts in this book have been obtained from a variety of sources. Clearly, some books on Gloucestershire's ghosts and legends have already been published and it would be remiss not to include some of the more interesting and relevant accounts contained within them. Privately printed, obscure and out-of-print publications were also consulted, along with numerous newspaper reports. In some cases, websites proved invaluable sources, but much of the material came from personal testimony provided by the many individuals who volunteered information. These are too numerous to name individually, but I offer my grateful thanks to everyone who took the time and trouble to share their experiences with me. I do wish, however, to acknowledge the following individuals, who have been especially helpful to me: Mary Boddington, David Day, David and Louise Duruty de Lloyd, Carol East, Oliver Lovell and Guy Stapleton.

All pictures courtesy of the author unless stated otherwise.

Mark Turner, 2011

GAZETTEER OF MYSTERIOUS GLOUCESTERSHIRE

ALDSWORTH

This quiet little village, between Northleach and Burford, lies a couple of miles or so off the busy A40 road. It is attractive enough, with the small Norman Church of St Bartholomew standing on a hill above the village stream. The church has a spire, which is unusual in the Cotswolds, and an imposing display of grotesque gargoyles that face visitors as they approach along the path. Included among these are dragons, grimacing faces and strange

creatures – all no doubt with their origins in myths and legends. Quite why such an impressive display was created at this small church is unclear.

About a mile and a half to the north-west of the village is Lodge Park, originally the deer park of nearby Sherborne House. Intended as a stone grandstand for deer coursing spectators, the Lodge itself was built in 1634 for Sir John 'Crump' Dutton, who had inherited the Sherborne estate sixteen years earlier. Known as 'Crump' because of his hunchback, Dutton has been described as a 'cunning rogue' and had two marriages to wealthy heiresses. He was a member of parliament in the early parliaments of King Charles I and, although very rich,

Lodge Park entrance gates, Aldsworth.

Lodge Park, Aldsworth.

apparently refused to pay the forced loan demanded by the King in 1625 – ending up in gaol for his trouble. 'Crump' was also, it is said, inclined to double-dealing during the English Civil war, backing both sides in the troubles. His actions were in due course revealed and, according to legend, a curse was laid in Parliament upon the Duttons to the effect that in the twentieth century the last member of the family would die. Whether this colourful yarn is simply invention is not known, but it is beyond dispute that in the 1980s an elderly Dutton spinster died, leaving no heir to the name. 'Crump' died in 1657 and a memorial to him may be seen in Sherborne Church. The ghostly spectre of a somewhat inebriated 'Crump' is said to have been seen travelling in a phantom coach and horses that drives through the ornate gates at the entrance of Lodge Park.

Lodge Park has other mysterious accounts surrounding it, too. The place is said to possess a 'vanished' room, which resulted from a practice that was common in the Northleach area many years ago. A troublesome ghost would be exorcised by priests and sealed in a barrel, which would then be placed in a little-used room – masons and carpenters blocking all doors and windows so that the ghost could not be accidentally released. Such rooms came to be known as 'vanished' rooms.

There have been reports of poltergeist activity at one of the entrance lodges at the gates to Lodge Park, and once a spectral white stag was seen moving noiselessly across the approach to the house before passing straight through a dense hedge. A little to the south of Lodge Park the road runs past Larkethill Wood, and there are stories of a ghostly coach and four horses having been seen careering down the hill and around the corner at the bottom, before disappearing from view. Is this the ghostly re-enactment of some dreadful accident from many years ago?

Situated around six miles to the east of Aldsworth is the Oxfordshire town of Burford, its surrounding fields and woods reputedly home to 'The Beast of Burford' – thought by many to be a black panther-like big cat. Several people claim to have seen the cat, and it is thought to be responsible for killing a number of sheep. Keepers at the Cotswold Wildlife Park, just a couple of miles from Burford, believe the 'beast' was responsible for killing one of their Indian Blackbucks, owing to the severe mauling it received. It may be that 'The Beast of Burford' trespassed into Gloucestershire in 2005, when an Aldsworth farmer saw what he described as 'a huge black cat' at his farm.

AMBERLEY

Mysterious activity in Amberley seems confined to the village's two inns. Standing on a commanding hillside position, and enjoying fine views over the Woodchester Valley, the nineteenth-century Amberley Inn has a long tradition as the haunt of notorious highwayman Tom Long. It is said that he fell in love with the landlord's daughter, but his amorous intentions were thwarted when the landlord – perhaps understandably – forbade his daughter from seeing Long. It is claimed that the highwayman was subsequently hanged, for his crimes, at a spot on Minchinhampton Common, today marked by a signpost known as 'Tom Long's Post'.

There have for many years been reports of ghostly activity at The Amberley Inn, though whether the highwayman is really the source is open to doubt. One fairly recent account describes how a guest staying at the inn was taking a bath one evening when he became overwhelmed by a 'feeling of dread'. Enquiries revealed, it is said, that years earlier a man had committed suicide in the bathroom by cutting his wrists; this tragic act apparently accounting for the awful atmosphere sensed by the guest. Staff members, too, have reported peculiar activity in the building, with objects such as keys and pillowcases going missing and taps and switches turning on and off of their own accord. On one occasion a guest awoke with the feeling that he was not alone. A nearby bed showed the indentation of a figure although there was no one else in the room, and when a female member of staff subsequently slept there she found herself unable to move the bedding because some unseen figure in the bed was hogging the blankets. Sceptical readers might wonder whether this staff member's loneliness in bed led her to dream that someone was sharing it with her.

The Black Horse Inn, too, apparently has a resident ghost. The landlord was, before becoming licensee at the inn, a complete sceptic in-so-far as accounts of ghosts are concerned, but regular inexplicable noises have led him to think again. The distinct sounds of footsteps, coughing, and the noises made by someone moving around, have on several occasions been heard when there was no person in the vicinity – or, perhaps one should say, no *living* person in the vicinity.

AMPNEY CRUCIS

A strange structure from the fourteenth century stands in the village churchyard. Thought to be a 'weeping cross' where 'penitents resorted to bemoan over their shortcomings', the head of this peculiar stone erection was only rediscovered in 1854 after being found in the rood loft of the church. It is probable that the head had been hidden there to prevent its destruction by image destroyers active during the Cromwellian period. Obscure in origin, such crosses are rare in England.

AMPNEY ST PETER

One of the strangest features of this village is a small figure carved into a stone wall near the font in the village church. The figure is that of a nude female, and it would at one time have been quite graphic in its depiction of the naked body, although observers with voyeuristic tendencies will be disappointed to find that the carving has at some time been defaced, obliterating the quasi-erotic anatomical display.

Such figures are known as Sheela-na-Gigs, the origin of the name being the subject of some dispute. In general, however, it is thought to mean 'immoral hag or old woman'. Most of the figures date from the twelfth century, and although they are usually explained as 'pagan fertility symbols' their purpose is actually something of a mystery. One theory suggests they represent a Celtic goddess, while another explains the figures as a warning against lust and the sins of the flesh. Yet another theory describes them as a protection against evil – the somewhat unlikely notion being that demons and devils might be repelled by the sight of a woman's genitalia.

Defaced Sheela-na-Gig, St Peter's Church, Ampney St Peter.

If the condition of the female figure in the church is anything to judge by, Ampney St. Peter's puritans of yesteryear preferred to take their chances with demons than with exhibitionist ladies.

aRLINGHam

Several accounts of ghosts and spectres are centred on this small village close to the River Severn. A lady visiting the village church in 1902 to view some carvings saw a woman in black seated in one of the pews, and asked her where the carvings were located. The old woman smiled, apparently, then immediately vanished, yet was seen a little later to be back in the pew. When, subsequently, the description of the apparition was given to the church gardener he volunteered the view that it was the ghost of the vicar's housekeeper who had been dead for some years.

Another house in the village is said to be home to a ghostly lady. One occupant of Slowwe House reported seeing a lady in a long grey dress and a grey bonnet in the courtyard in 1970. Moments later, it was noticed that the figure had disappeared. Children of the household also claimed to have seen the grey lady in their bedroom, although the evidence to support this ghost story is rather flimsy.

Probably the best story from Arlingham is recounted by author Rupert Matthews in his book *Haunted Gloucestershire*. This tale concerns a ghostly funeral cortege that, it is said, was seen to form up outside the church before proceeding through the village and halting outside the front door of Arlingham Manor. Matthews describes how the driver of the phantom hearse drew up his horses and turned to gaze 'with baleful eye upon the house'. The sighting of this ghostly procession was thought to be a portent of misfortune in the household, and there were many stories of how it was seen trundling up to the house. In 1757, particularly, several villagers claimed to have seen the spectral cortège, and when a few members of the family fell ill and died exactly a year later its portentous purpose must have been considered virtually proven. The house has been gone for years, however, and now all that remains is the dovecote.

aSTON maGNa

Although only a small village, Aston Magna seems to have had more than its fair share of peculiar happenings, with stories of apparitions, poltergeists and a monster that attacked a resident's pet cat. Even the village's original name of Hanging Aston lends the place a somewhat foreboding air of mystery. It has been suggested that the name is a corruption of Hengen Aston and refers to some ancient and obscure earthworks in fields to the south of the now-redundant village church. The earthworks are themselves something of a mystery, and although usually regarded as the remains of a moat, that surrounded a long-vanished castle or homestead, it has been suggested that the site is actually a Neolithic-henge monument.

Newland Farm, Aston Magna.

Unexplained rapping sounds have been heard in a house on the village High Street and in the 1960s a shadowy figure was frequently seen passing up a stairway at Norton Cottage. At Aston Magna Manor many years ago the sounds of someone moving about in the loft of the adjacent coach-house were so audible that the police were summoned. When the village policeman arrived from nearby Blockley, he heard the noises for himself and together with the householder went up to confront the intruder. Upon entering the loft, however, the officer found no one present and the noises stopped. Elsewhere in the village ghostly noises have been heard, with male voices singing in prayer apparently being heard at the ancient Norman Chapel (a cottage since about 1604), and at night the haunting cries of a baby have been heard coming from the garden of a house in Church View.

A bend in the road that leads to the neighbouring village of Draycott is well known locally as being the haunt of a ghostly lady dressed all in white. This story goes back many years, and whether the ghost has been seen in recent times is not known. The bend has, however, long been known as 'Lady On Corner'. This is undoubtedly a case of local legend embellishing accounts that have been handed down over the years. A first-hand account has, however, been given about the regular sighting of a monk-like apparition at the fifteenth-century Newland Farm in Aston Magna. A former resident of the building has described how, in the 1960s, he and his sister often saw the hooded and cloaked figure drift across a wall, near the ceiling of their bedroom. Apparently the figure would remain for several minutes at a time, before fading from view. The apparition always appeared at night and on several occasions the children even moved furniture in the room in case something was casting an eerie shadow.

The final account from the village is one that, on the face of it, rather stretches credibility. It comes from Woollaway Bungalows, close to Church View, and concerns a monster-like creature. In the late 1980s the occupant of one of the bungalows was in her home when she saw her pet cat begin to step through the cat flap in the outside door, then watched in horror as a claw 'the size of a man's hand' lunged through the flap and pinned the cat to the door. Injured, the cat struggled frenziedly, eventually extricating itself from the vice-like grip. As soon as the cat had been released, its owners opened the door and rushed out, half-expecting to see something like a panther or leopard. No such animal was seen, however, although the grass nearby was flattened and the ground bore footprints 'like a bear's', suggesting that the unwanted visitor had been something very large. Indeed, recently received information suggests that this account may not be as incredible as it first seems. A long-standing resident of Aston Magna has stated that it is 'well known' in the village that a panther is seen from time to time near the railway line.

AVENING

There is much in Avening to interest the historian and it is probably unsurprising that legend and mystery surround one of the village's antiquities. On the edge of the Gatcombe Park estate are the remains of a Neolithic burial mound, which has a stone known as 'The Tingle Stone' standing at its north end. Some 6ft high, this stone could be all that remains of a burial chamber, although it may have been placed in isolation, perhaps as a very overt barrier to the tomb. Local legend has it that the stone dances around the field when it hears the church clock strike midnight. The origin of the stone's name is not known, but dowsers operating nearby have reported experiencing tingling sensations such as might be associated with mild electric shocks.

Other objects of mystery and curiosity are the enigmatic 'green men'. Two of these ancient pagan symbols are to be seen in the nave and chancel of the church at Avening. These images of the human form, sprouting or swathed in foliage, are generally considered to represent fertility and regeneration and, although very much connected with paganism and folklore, are widely found in Christian churches. Why, one may ask, has the church long permitted this pagan symbol to inhabit its places of Christian worship? Canon Albert Radcliffe's preface to *The Green Man* by Clive Hicks provides some food for thought, suggesting that the green man represents the sins of the flesh, or is 'representative of pagan and natural human nature, witnessing to Christ, and thereby redeemed and brought into the service of the gospel'. In the absence of any firm evidence, however, this can only be educated conjecture.

Below the red cliff at Gatcombe is a house known locally as Drake's House. It was once lived in by Sir Francis Drake and there is a story that his bearded figure has been seen there at dusk. Seated in an armchair, he gazes westwards along the river, then, as dusk falls, his figure fades from view. This evocative tale is thought to originate from the nineteenth century, and there is certainly no recent report of the apparition being seen.

The phantom of a lady in a long dress is said to have been seen by motorists on the road between Avening and Minchinhampton. No doubt she seems perfectly lifelike, for it is only when drivers stop to offer assistance that her less-than-earthly presence is revealed and the figure, it is said, completely vanishes. Almost nothing is known of this lady, as is the case of the ghost at The Cross Inn at Avening. Known to staff and patrons as 'William', he has for some years been resident in the pub cellar. One could easily think of worse places to haunt.

BAGENDON

Ancient earth ramparts and ditches known as Bagendon Dykes enclose an area of around 200 acres to the south and west of this village. These are the remains of the Celtic tribal capital of the Dobunni tribe, who ruled much of Gloucestershire in the Iron Age, before the arrival of the Romans.

A chieftain of that period is said to be buried at Bagendon Downs, south-west of the church, and it has long been believed that after dark he haunts the area. There seems to be no report of any recent sighting, although someone was fortunate to get a good look at him once – Rupert Matthews in *Haunted Gloucestershire* states that 'the ghost … carries with him a beautiful shield glittering with polished metal … and wields a sword…'

BAUNTON

J.A. Brooks, in his book *Ghosts and Witches of the Cotswolds*, makes reference to an odd occurrence said to have taken place in Baunton in 1646. A liquid the colour of blood is said to have suddenly risen out of an old table '…all that afternoone and the nighte following till the next day…'.

Rather more recently, however, a couple driving their car at Baunton reported seeing what may have been some kind of alien cat. The sighting took place in the 1990s, the cat being estimated at more than 3ft long, and having 'dark tabby colouring and a long ringed tail'. The husband suspected it might have been a young cheetah, although his wife thought it looked more like a European wild cat. Its presence there remains something of a mystery.

BERKELEY

The twelfth-century Berkeley Castle is reputedly home to Gloucestershire's most famous ghost – that of the murdered King Edward II. A very unpopular king, Edward was incompetent at running the state's financial affairs and presided over the military disaster at

Berkeley Castle, seen through the Gatehouse.   *King Edward II's effigy, Gloucester Cathederal.*

Bannockburn in 1314. Additionally, he was reputedly homosexual and tales of the favours granted to his male lovers were widespread. In 1327 his wife, Queen Isabella, working with her lover Roger Mortimer, the Earl of March, deposed the King and he was imprisoned at Berkeley Castle. It was not long, however, before he tried to escape, and, before the year was out, Roger Mortimer hatched a particularly cruel plan to dispose of Edward in a way that would leave no obvious mark to indicate foul play.

The popular legend is that Edward was weighted down by a mattress and murdered when his captors introduced a red-hot poker through a metal tube into his rectum, burning his bowel and intestines. It is little wonder that the king's screams of agony were reputedly heard for some distance around Berkeley. It has been claimed that even to the present day his screams and tortured wails can sometimes be heard emanating from the castle, and there are additional reports that the king's ghostly funeral procession is very occasionally seen leaving the castle and heading for Gloucester.

After the king's death was announced his body was placed in a tomb in Gloucester Abbey (now the cathedral). Isabella and Mortimer did not rule for very long – when Edward III came to the throne he had his mother retire from public life and saw to it that Mortimer was executed. He then had Edward's tomb replaced with the magnificent structure that exists today. The face of the alabaster effigy of the king is said to have been modelled from his death mask.

A second story, which originates from a folk-tale told over the centuries, concerns a woman known as the 'Witch of Berkeley'. This woman was known locally for her ability to tell fortunes and interpret omens. Even more sinister, she had a raven as a pet. One day, so the story goes, the bird took to the air, flew three times around the room then fell down dead. Clearly troubled by the bird's demise, the woman uttered the words, 'now this day is the plough come to my last furrow'. No sooner had she said this than a messenger came into the house and declared that her son and his family were dead. She, too, then fell ill.

The woman sent for her remaining children, who fortunately happened to be monks and nuns. From her deathbed she confessed that she had been 'a wicked follower of an evil art' and that she desired to be eased from her torment. She requested that her body be sewed in the skin of a stag and placed inside a stone chest that must be bound with three iron chains. Psalms had then to be sung over the body for forty days and forty nights. If, after three days, her body remained undisturbed then she was to be buried in the churchyard.

But, alas, it was not to be. Demons attacked the stone chest, breaking two of the chains, and on the third night the Devil himself arrived on the scene. He broke open the chest, commanded the dead body of the Witch of Berkeley to rise, then threw her over his black horse (waiting patiently outside the church) and galloped off.

The reference to a stag's skin has been suggested as having its origins in a pagan ritual, and the number three has long been considered sacred. Despite these possibly pagan connections, however, it is quite likely that monks were the original tellers of this tale, the aim being to discourage people from placing their faith in evil forces.

Finally, the parish church has a peculiar sculpture of a large toad with the heads of two children beneath it. This toad is supposed to have devoured two of the children of one of the lords of Berkeley. Apparently it developed a liking for human flesh and grew to a monstrous size by feeding on the bodies of prisoners who died in Berkeley Castle's *oubliette* (a dungeon with a trapdoor at the top). This odd sculpture can be seen at the top of the fourth pillar eastwards on the south side of the church. The official guide to the church makes no mention of the toad's flesh-eating reputation, however, describing the sculpture as 'a sermon in stone to teach that gossip is like the poisonous tongue of a toad'.

BIBURY

The village of Bibury, standing beside the pretty River Coln, has for many years been a popular tourist destination. It has a number of interesting features, including the seventeenth-century Arlington Mill, the setting for a tragic ghost story of jealousy and betrayal. According to the story, the mill was at one time lived in by a wealthy miller and his four adult sons, his wife having died some time previously. In due course, however, he married a young Bibury girl named Mary.

Astute readers will have already guessed the trouble brewing. The young wife and the eldest son fell in love and an affair began. The miller found out, however, and in a fight with the son threw him from the mill into the stream below, where he met his death. Despite the fact that it was a freezing January, with snow on the ground, the miller heaved his wife outside, paying no heed to her desperate pleas to be allowed back in. She was subsequently found on the banks of the River Coln, frozen to death. Some say that Mary's grey ghost is still seen near the mill.

Other spectres and apparitions that enthusiasts may like to be aware of are said to appear occasionally in the vicinity of Quarry Hill. A white woman leading a white ox is the restless ghost of Juliana, a woman excommunicated from the church centuries ago, while a ghostly coach and horses is supposed to appear each Christmas Eve, following a fatal accident in the late eighteenth century. The horses bolted, so the story goes, at the sight of a spectral funeral procession led by Juliana and her ox, the grey lady, and other lost souls.

These rather fanciful stories have no doubt been embroidered over the years and, by comparison, the ghostly 'customer' at The Catherine Wheel public house in the village

Arlington Mill, Bibury.

seems relatively prosaic. Staff members have on a number of occasions seen the apparition of a lady sitting in a corner of the lounge bar. Although completely harmless and benign, the ghost seems to dislike change, becoming somewhat mischievous in recent years when redecoration was taking place. Various items were inexplicably moved about and doors were seen to open, apparently of their own accord. There is always the possibility, of course, that the ghost is that of poor Mary visiting for some warmth before continuing her efforts to regain entry to Arlington Mill.

BIRDLIP

Standing on the edge of the Cotswolds, its great beech woods looking over the Severn Valley, this village's name derives from bird or bride's leap. The area around Birdlip Hill might be thought by some to be rather lonely, so it is just as well that the ghostly black dog said to haunt the hill is considered benevolent. In her book *The Folklore of the Cotswolds* Katharine M. Briggs states the dog is 'a helpful spirit who guides lost travellers'. In the 1990s, however, a motorist fleetingly saw a 'beast' at the top of Birdlip Hill. Close to the side of the road was a large black cat, estimated to be nearly 3ft long – 4ft including the tail. Unsurprisingly, the motorist did not stop to investigate further.

In Buckle Wood, off the road between Birdlip and Stroud, is West Tump long barrow – a Neolithic burial mound of the sort constructed around 4-5,000 years ago. It was excavated in the nineteenth century, revealing at least a dozen skeletons, one of which was thought to be that of a young woman, with a baby lying close by. The excavators considered this person to have been a Cotswold chieftain. In his book *Paranormal Cotswolds*, author Anthony Poulton-Smith relates a tale of how a rambler saw an unusual group of four men standing on top of the mound. Looking very much like one might suppose people of the New Stone Age to have appeared, these characters each held a spear and wore 'breeches or skirts of leather or coarse cloth'. Poulton-Smith wonders whether these men – bare-chested and with hair that was 'wild and naturally curly' – were mourning the death of the woman and child. The unusual image faded after a few moments, but it is pleasing to note that apparitional Neolithic warriors can now be numbered among the ghostly monks, highwaymen and white ladies more commonly seen in the county.

BISHOP'S CLEEVE

The ancient and mysterious image of the 'green man', so widely seen throughout Gloucestershire and beyond, makes an appearance on a capital of the south porch of the Church of St Michael and Angels in the village. Does he represent fertility and regeneration, as is widely thought? Whatever his purpose, he certainly presents an interesting image to ponder over. Two carved beasts resembling dragons or serpents are carved above the arch of the inner doorway. Each beast is swallowing another beaked creature or bird.

Left: *Dragon at Bishop's Cleeve Church.*

Below: *'Green Man' at Bishop's Cleeve Church.*

Other mysterious aspects of Bishop's Cleeve are of ghostly origin. Roy Palmer, in his book *Folklore of Gloucestershire*, describes how a cyclist dressed in clothing reminiscent of the 1930s was seen in the 1980s riding down the hill from Southam towards Prestbury. This apparitional figure may have been connected with an accident that took place at the location some fifty years earlier.

The bar of Bishop's Cleeve's ancient pub, The Royal Oak, is apparently the focal point for occasional paranormal occurrences. The building is believed to date from 1597 and, as with most buildings of such age, the creaking sounds of ancient timbers settling are probably not uncommon. Whether such minuscule movement provides a plausible explanation of how a pint of beer was once seen to slide off the bar counter, apparently of its own accord, seems unlikely. Additionally, shadowy forms have sometimes been fleetingly seen in the bar area, leading to a belief that the building is haunted.

BISLEY

This fairly large village a little to the north of Stroud, with narrow streets and pretty stone houses, is full of interest. The church has a splendid steeple, and although the building is probably Anglo-Saxon in origin it was extensively restructured in the 1860s. During this time two Roman altars were excavated near the tower, supporting a theory that the church may have been built upon the site of a Roman temple (the altars are now in the British Museum). There are various interesting features inside the building, including an early fourteenth-century effigy of a knight, whose identity is a mystery. Indeed, the construction of the building is itself cloaked in a degree of mystery and folklore if an old tale is to be believed. The story goes that when the building was completed at a site about a mile from where it stands today the Devil demolished it and moved it to its current location.

Perhaps it was the Devil in canine form that confronted a couple in the grounds of the church one damp afternoon in the early years of the twenty-first century. As the couple came out of the building they were faced with a very large dog with a 'black coat and dark, burnt red eyes' and a 'wet, drool-smeared mouth'. The beast twice barked at the couple, yet, although its mouth was seen to make barking motions, not a sound was heard. The couple quickly turned and took a few paces back to the church, but on turning back to look for the dog saw that it had completely vanished.

Mysterious occurrences have taken place at a couple of Bisley's other burial sites, although in these cases the graves are thousands of years old. Off Hayhedge Lane, to the east of the village, are the scanty remnants of the Giant's Stone long barrow. Actually, there is no trace of the barrow itself, with the broken remains of two of the burial chamber stones just about visible to determined explorers. Apparently, reports exist of a headless horseman having been seen riding past the location, although this is thought to be a very old tale.

More widely reported, however, is a story connected with Money Tump – a Bronze Age round barrow situated beside a track running south from Bisley to France Lynch.

In 1912 a group of men were returning to Bisley, having been to a fair at France Lynch, when they saw a number of figures standing at Money Tump and assumed them to be members of the group who had gone ahead. Calls went unheeded and, as they drew nearer, they saw to their horror that the figures were headless phantoms. This story has been told many times and, indeed, accounts do vary somewhat. It has been suggested that the figures may not have been headless, but had their heads bowed in prayer – and there is always the faint possibility, of course, that the group attending the fair had perhaps been a little over-enthusiastic in their consumption of ale.

BLOCKLEY

Residents in the village of Blockley were perplexed when in 1981 a hole some 15ft across and up to 70ft deep suddenly opened up in a field off Greenway Road. A farm worker was driving a combine harvester in the field at the time and was fortunate not to fall into the great pit that was revealed. Its purpose remains a mystery, however, and, as it was filled in before it could be examined by either geological or historical experts, suggestions that it might have been the remains of a medieval stone quarry or a well are mere conjecture. There are no buildings anywhere near the site, so even the possibility that it might have been evidence of a secret tunnel or subterranean passage seems remote. A couple of dwellings in the area have been the focal point for poltergeist activity. A couple staying in a cottage close to Hangman's Hall Farm in the early 1970s claimed to have had their sleep disrupted by inexplicable noises, windows opening apparently of their own accord, and ghostly footsteps. On one occasion the marital bed even began moving about unaided, which cynical readers may feel is rather reminiscent of 1973 horror movie *The Exorcist*. In any event, the couple moved on and were untroubled in their new home.

In 1977 a house on the Winterway estate was the scene of various paranormal disturbances. Within days of occupying the house, an apparitional figure was seen independently by several members of the family. Soon afterwards, the family found their sleep disrupted by rapping sounds, and windows were opened by some unseen force. Further, they would awake in the morning to find various items, such as keys and slippers, strewn around the floor. It is unsurprising, then, that they quickly moved home.

Spectral black dogs are not uncommon in Gloucestershire, and a Blockley resident has reported seeing such an animal in the late 1960s or early 1970s. The witness was walking home one evening past The Crown Inn when he saw a black dog walking ahead of him towards Dovedale Woods. He followed it for some distance, apparently, then, as he watched it, the dog completely vanished. Although it had seemed real enough, it did not have opportunity to dart into any nearby garden, claimed the witness – and he philosophically accepts it must have been an apparition.

Rumours of big cats being seen in the area have occasionally circulated, too, although it seems such stories are invariably based on mistaken identification. As recently as 2010 a feline beast 'the size of a Labrador' was apparently seen attacking a domestic cat in the vicinity of the High Street. The fate of the cat is not known but, in the absence of any report to the contrary, it is assumed that it made good its escape.

BOURTON-ON-THE-HILL

The north Cotswolds area is rich in antiquities from our ancient ancestors, with barrows and earthworks widely distributed across the district. Many of the burial mounds have been excavated – sometimes in a rather rough-and-ready fashion – to reveal the presence of skeletal remains, although a number of barrows appear to have escaped the enthusiastic attentions of Victorian archaeologists. Often, these ancient burial mounds have a sombre air of mystery and intrigue about them – particularly where they remain undisturbed – and folklore beliefs have sometimes built up around them. One such barrow is the Neolithic long barrow situated near to Tower View Farm, off the Sezincote Lane at Bourton-on-the-Hill. There is no record of archaeological examination of the barrow ever having taken place, so how many bodies are contained within it remains unknown. It has been reported that children living nearby believed that, years ago, a rope and noose were suspended from a tree growing on the barrow, from which criminals were hanged. The likelihood of hangings having taken place at the long barrow is remote, although it is believed that a gallows once stood at nearby Troopers Lodge, which may be the source of the tale.

BOURTON-ON-THE-WATER

An apparitional motorcycle and sidecar has been seen in this popular village, according to author Rupert Matthews. In his book *Haunted Gloucestershire* he describes how this 'phantom motorbike' passes by in silence – tending to support the suspicion that it is an apparition. One motorist, apparently, saw it vanish into thin air.

Beside the River Windrush, which flows through the village, stands The Old Manse Hotel – built in 1748 for the local Baptist pastor, as a reward for his services to the community. Anthony Poulton-Smith, in his book *Paranormal Cotswolds*, describes how the hotel is believed to be haunted by a benign ghost named 'George'. No one has reported actually having heard or seen him, however, with his presence merely being 'sensed'. George, it is said, hanged himself in the building – though when, and for what reason, is a mystery.

BROAD CAMPDEN

This charming village, with its stone cottages and thatched roofs, is not without its tales of mystery. 'Black Shuck' is a name given to a large black demon-dog, with flaming red eyes, that has apparently been seen in the lanes around Broad Campden from time to time. Ghostly black dogs are actually commonly reported, although the legend of 'Black Shuck' is more usually associated with East Anglia, and quite when Broad Campden's hound was most recently seen is not known.

The Malt House, Broad Campden.

In the 1960s the hazy figure of a man, with a dog by his side, was seen by two girls in the road outside Broad Campden's seventeenth-century Malt House. Glowing with a whitish light, the figure was clearly not that of a living person, and the girls ran away in fear. The apparitional dog was certainly no 'Black Shuck', though, and the girls subsequently learned that the ghost was believed to be that of a man who had committed suicide, after first killing his pet dog.

Quite near to The Malt House, and behind a high wall and hedge, is the village's Norman Chapel House. The place consists of a chapel dated 1130 and a fifteenth-century priest's house, and stood derelict until it was converted into a dwelling in the early years of the twentieth century. It is a private house, not open to the public, but there have been reports of the ghostly figures of cloaked and hooded monks having been seen many times, especially in the gardens.

BROADWELL

A very pleasant walk along an old bridle path can be taken between Broadwell and nearby Stow-on-the-Wold, although those with superstitious tendencies might do well to bear in mind accounts of a ghostly lady seen there many times over the years. The lady – dressed in black and carrying an open umbrella – was always seen at dusk, walking slowly towards Stow, and the weather on each occasion was fine, rendering the umbrella's use unnecessary. Whenever spoken to, the figure vanished – no one ever passed the lady, nor met her face to face. She has, though, not been seen for some years. On one occasion another figure was seen – this time close to where the path meets the road. A motorist was startled when a figure dressed in costume of the Civil War period stepped out in front of his car, although the sighting was only momentary and there was no collision. There was in fact much activity in the area during the Civil War, with the final battle of the conflict taking place at nearby Donnington in 1646.

The apparition of a lady was seen by a woman in a house named Shenley in the centre of the village in the late 1970s. The figure was not in any way frightening, however, so the

Bridle path to Stow, Broadwell.

The Fox Inn, Broadwell.

woman quickly disregarded it. Then, some ten years later, she was shown a photograph of a former occupant of the house, and the image perfectly matched that of the apparition seen years before.

The village pub, The Fox, is a very welcoming place, where people tend to return again and again. As with many pubs and hotels, the place is reported to have a resident ghost, and although sceptics often regard haunted pubs

The Fox Inn, Broadwell. Ghostly apparition or photographic anomaly? (Photo courtesy of Alan B. Sams P.A.)

as particularly open to suspicion the paranormal activity at The Fox does seem rather more persistent than at many locations. Suspected to be the mischievous ghost of a former landlord, the spook's antics include disrupting cutlery laid neatly on tables for diners, causing doors to open of their own accord, pacing around rooms when it was known that no living person was there, and even causing the distinctive smell of pipe-tobacco to waft through the bar when not open to the public. At least one person claims to have seen an apparition seated in the bar, accompanied by a sensation of intense cold. Of particular curiosity is a digital photograph taken in the bar in late 2008. The picture was taken by a tourist, purely to illustrate the empty bar, decorated with a Christmas tree. When printed, however, the photograph showed a faint, but quite discernible, image of two figures near the tree. This may be merely a curious optical effect caused by movement of the camera, or perhaps the blurry images are those of the ghostly former landlord and a customer.

CERNEY WICK

This village close to the Cotswold Water Park has a seventeenth-century stone inn, apparently haunted by the ghost of an elderly man. The Crown Inn, popular with both drinkers and diners, was extended in the twentieth century, but staff members have reported unusual activity in the original part of the building, where the public bar is situated.

Heavy, deliberate footsteps have been heard crossing an upper floor when it was known that no one was there, and more than one person has become suddenly aware of an intense cold feeling. On one occasion a woman was unnerved when she inexplicably felt the sensation of 'breath' on her neck. The ghost has even made a visible appearance, too, with the landlady once seeing the apparition of an old man wearing a flat cap.

CHALFORD

An ancient story of love and tragedy is said to account for sightings of an apparition at Chalford's Gypsy Lane. A young woman who worked for a wealthy farmer in Chalford fell in love with his son, and they met secretly near a stile in the corner of a field adjoining the lane. It seems that these stile-side meetings led to passionate exchanges and, unfortunately, she became pregnant. The son rejected her upon learning the news and, unable to stand life without him, she hanged herself in a nearby barn. This tragic tale is claimed to date back to the seventeenth century. Some 300 years later, however, when the RAF were stationed nearby, several airmen reported seeing a young woman – dressed in clothes of a bygone era – waiting at the stile and staring into the distance. When approached, it was said, the young woman vanished. Although a good story, with perhaps some basis in truth, this account is so old that it can only be regarded as folklore.

Far more contemporary (but also rather less of a tale) are reports that a former regular patron, now deceased, of The Old Neighbourhood Inn seems more reluctant than most to move on to pastures new. His apparition has been seen gliding through a solid wall in the pub and a bathroom light that switches on of its own accord has been attributed to his activities.

CHARFIELD

A particularly sad tale comes from this village near the southern edge of the Cotswolds. The main railway line from Gloucester to Bristol passes beneath a bridge in Charfield, and it was here in the early morning on 13 October 1928 that a collision involving three trains took place. It was scarcely surprising when, in those days of gas-lit wooden railway carriages, the wreckage quickly became a raging inferno, resulting in the loss of fifteen lives. Two of those who died were never identified and, even though the small size of the bodies suggested they were children, no one ever came forward to claim them.

The precise cause of the crash was never established, although it seemed clear that either driver or signalling error was to blame. More of a mystery, however, is how the two 'Charfield Railway Children' have remained unnamed. Indeed, on a granite memorial cross in a nearby churchyard they are simply listed as 'two unknown'. Various theories have been put forward over the years, although none has seemed convincing. It was suggested that that they might actually have been jockeys rather than children, and in 1937 a London woman claimed the bodies were those of her two young brothers. This claim was dismissed, as were far-fetched suggestions that the bodies were somehow connected with a senior local police officer, or were in fact a ventriloquist's dummies. Until the 1950s an elderly woman dressed in black was seen to visit the grave two or three times a year, although no one ever spoke to her and her identity is unknown. Folklore and legend has gathered over the years in efforts to explain the mystery, and there have been occasional reports of two ghostly children seen walking hand in hand near the site of the accident.

CHEDWORTH

This large and attractive village scattered along the steep-sided valley of the River Coln is probably best known for its splendid Roman villa, which is in the care of The National Trust. The church and stone cottages are very attractive, too, and the village pub, The Seven Tuns Inn, has a very good reputation for the quality of its cuisine.

Many visit the pub for its live music evenings, too, although stories of the ghosts apparently seen there are probably less well known. A regular user of the place, who is now deceased, is supposed to have been seen in the skittle alley and, in 2007, a photograph taken inside the pub showed only the ghostly image of a mouth and a pair of eyes.

CHELTENHAM

This handsome spa town, with its tree-lined promenade and elegant Georgian houses, might at first glance look rather too grand to be a likely setting for tales of mystery and suspense. However, there are a number of such tales, including accounts of persistent ghosts, an infamous 'torso murder', and numerous sightings of unidentified flying objects.

Probably one of Cheltenham's earliest tales concerns the legend of Maud's Elm. As with so many legends, the tale has no doubt been embellished over the years, but it is probable that much of it is based on events that actually happened. The story starts in an area known as Swindon – once a village separate from the town, but today a suburb without much identity of its own – which is situated on the northern edge of the built-up area. If one takes the road – Swindon Road – towards the town centre, one comes upon a small roundabout at its junction with Richards Road and Malvern Street, and it is at this spot that a wicked act of cruelty and injustice occurred hundreds of years ago.

A young woman named Maud Bowen from Swindon village had one day gone into Cheltenham, but by night had not returned, so a search was made for her. Her lifeless body was found, alas, drowned in nearby Wyman's Brook. She was naked and appeared to have been raped. Another body was soon found, however, this time that of the girl's uncle, Godrey. He had been killed by an arrow through the heart, and his hand still clutched a strip of young Maud's clothing. The assumption was that Godrey had raped his niece, and that – distraught and shamed – Maud had committed suicide by throwing herself into the brook. Godfrey's fatal injury was, apparently, attributed to the work of God.

Maud's body was buried at a nearby crossroads, the stake of a living elm tree thrust through her heart and into the ground. (This bizarre method of burial was commonly used in cases of suicide.) The stake subsequently grew into a tree known as Maud's Elm. Maud's elderly mother, Margaret, was stricken with grief and took to wandering the roads around the area, often being seen, it is said, sobbing at her daughter's burial place. On one such occasion she was seen by the lord of the manor, Sir Robert de Vere, who ordered his men to remove her from his sight. A man-at-arms hastened to move the old woman, but before he could do so, was slain by an arrow that shot out of a nearby thicket.

A search failed to find the person responsible, so poor Margaret was pronounced a witch and sentenced to death by burning at Maud's Elm. Sir Robert de Vere came to gloat as the old woman burned, but in an apparent act of justice some unseen person shot an arrow into his heart, causing him to fall dead onto the fire.

Many years later an old man, unrecognised by the villagers of Swindon, took to living in the house that had been home to Maud Bowen. It transpired that his name was Walter Gray and that he had been young Maud's sweetheart. Maud had been a very pretty woman, and was desired by Sir Robert de Vere and by her uncle, Godfrey. It seems that Godfrey and the lord of the manor plotted to rape and murder her, but that Walter chanced upon the girl's uncle carrying out the deed and shot him dead. De Vere ran off, as did Maud, but although the lord of the manor made good his escape, Maud fell into the brook and drowned. Walter subsequently kept watch over his sweetheart's mother, slaying the man-at-arms and de Vere.

Maud's Elm was apparently quite an attraction for the well-heeled people of Cheltenham during the eighteenth century, and it was not uncommon for them to make special visits to see it. In 1907, though, the great tree was struck by lightning and, severely damaged, had to be cut down. Now all that remains is a minor road junction and distant recollections of an ancient tale – the Legend of Maud's Elm.

As well as being the setting for a poignant legend, Cheltenham seems to be home to a number of ghosts. The best-evidenced case on record took place at St. Anne's House in Pittville Circus Road. Built in 1860, the house was first lived in by a couple named Swinhoe and in 1882 it was let to a Captain Despard, who changed the name of the house to 'Garden Reach'. Within months of moving into the house, the family became plagued by the frequent appearance of a ghost described as 'a tall lady in black'. This figure was seen by several – but not all – of the people who occupied the house and it became the

Maud's Elm, Cheltenham.

subject of an investigation by the Society for Psychical Research. One theory suggested that the figure was actually that of Captain Despard's mistress, yet it glided through threads placed to trap it, and simply vanished when pursued into a corner. It is difficult to imagine that even the most cunning of mistresses would be able to convincingly perform such feats. In any case, the figure was seen after the Despard family departed the house.

Initially the ghost had seemed solid and lifelike, but gradually became much less distinct and was not seen after 1889. A revival of the haunting occurred in 1903, however, when the ghost was seen several times in the garden, and when the house was used as a private school in the 1940s it closed because of 'constant ghost problems'. St Anne's

St Anne's, Pittville Circus Road, Cheltenham.

was eventually turned into flats, with one occupant frequently seeing and hearing a ghost in the building between 1957 and 1962. Little else seems to have been reported, although in 1979 a normally stable and calm dog became highly excited, running around and barking at nothing, when it came to live in the grounds of the house. One day the animal suffered a minor heart attack, which a vet attributed to shock. Interestingly, when the ghost's activity had been at its height dogs were on several occasions observed to react to it.

Overlooking the famous Cheltenham Racecourse is a Tudor manor house today occupied by the Hotel de la Bere. An apparition seen walking the corridors, and footsteps heard pacing in a room above the bar are attributed to the ghost of a matron at a girl's school, which once occupied the building. She came to a tragic end, it is said, when she hanged herself in the room above the bar.

It is probable that many of Cheltenham's hotels and pubs have some sort of ghost story connected with them, but some tales are better known than others. The story of the 'Tapping Maid' at The Suffolk Arms in Suffolk Road is quite well known. Tapping sounds have been heard in almost every room in the pub, but most especially in the cellar, and the figure of a young girl with a white apron has been seen in curious circumstances from time to time. All this activity is put down to a tragic accident that is believed to have occurred in the late 1800s, whereby a young girl was run over and killed in the cellar by a rolling beer barrel.

Everyman Theatre, Cheltenham.

The Leckhampton Inn at Cheltenham's Shurdington Road is haunted by a phantom dog, apparently. On various occasions a terrier dog has been seen gambolling around on the ground floor, before running off to an elderly man standing nearby. The man bends down as if to pat the dog and then the pair vanishes. No one seems to know the origin of the old man and his dog, but it is not beyond the realms of possibility that they were once regular visitors to the inn.

Fatal accidents are believed to be the cause of incidences of haunting at two of Cheltenham's best known places of entertainment. The Dress Circle at The Everyman Theatre in Regent Street is supposed to be haunted by the ghost of a builder who fell to his death during construction of the building in the late nineteenth century. Inexplicable noises, such as bumps and bangs – and even music coming from an empty stage – have been put down to the ghost.

Close by, in Imperial Square, is Cheltenham's handsome Town Hall, dated 1906. As at The Everyman Theatre, a man suffered a fatal fall from the balcony during the final stages of the hall's construction. Banging noises, unexpected chills and swinging lights are all claimed to be caused by the man's ghost, although a second fatality in the building – this time when a member of the public fell down the staircase in the 1960s – could just as easily be the source of the alleged paranormal activity. In yet another version of the haunting at least one employee at the building believes it connected with the untimely death of an American serviceman who, years ago, fell and 'bashed his brains out' on a pillar at the foot of the stairway. The staff room near the foot of the stairs, too, seems to be a focus for paranormal activity, and staff members have on numerous occasions seen the apparition of a lady in black in a corner of the room.

Untimely death is at the centre of another of Cheltenham's mysteries – although this involves a notorious murder case, in which – unlike accounts of ghosts and incidences of haunting – very tangible and grisly human remains feature prominently. The story began at Tirley on 10 January 1938, when local men found a canvas shoe and a glove lying on the footway of Haw Bridge. Bloodstains were seen on the horizontal rail and vertical iron supports, and what looked like small fragments of flesh were visible on the path. The police were called and the various items were taken to Gloucester Royal Infirmary, where they were examined by a pathologist. Interest faded, however, when the pathologist stated that he did not consider the blood to be human.

Interest was substantially revived when on 3 February two fishermen placed their net across the River Severn a little way downstream from Haw Bridge and found some spectacularly gruesome human remains. One of the men was immediately sick when it was seen that a swollen and putrefying male torso – the head, arms and legs had been roughly hacked off – had been caught in the net. Two bricks had been attached to the torso in an attempt to weigh it down in the water. The police soon arrived and the remains were taken to

Cheltenham Town Hall.

Cheltenham Hospital, and within a couple of days the Gloucestershire Constabulary called in Scotland Yard and renowned pathologist, Sir Bernard Spilsbury – who, after examining the remains, commented that they were those of a well-nourished middle-aged man.

A search was made in the river to try and find the missing body parts. A right arm – minus its hand – was found, then, a few days later, the two legs were found. Like the torso, bricks had been tied to the limbs. Police had meanwhile been making enquiries about missing middle-aged men and had found that a Captain William Butt, aged 55 years, had left his home at 248 Old Bath Road, Cheltenham and had not been seen since. Butt lived there with his wife, who was in poor health and needed constant care. She received this care from a private nurse, Irene Sullivan, who had a son, Brian, living in London. A somewhat insipid-looking character, Brian made a living as a dance-hall host with aspirations of becoming a professional dancer. He frequently came to stay with his mother in Cheltenham, spending his nights at Butt's Old Bath Road house, or at a place named Tower Lodge – situated almost opposite Daisy Bank Road on Cheltenham's Leckhampton Hill – lived in by his mother.

In December 1937 Brian Sullivan visited Cheltenham to spend Christmas with his mother. On 24 January 1938, having not heard from her son for a while – and having some days earlier seen newspapers blocking the letterbox to Tower Lodge – Irene Sullivan attended there and effected entry. She found her son dead in bed, apparently having taken

Stairway and staffroom entrance, Cheltenham Town Hall.

his own life. Captain Butt, meanwhile had gone missing from his house in Old Bath Road – although this was of little concern to Nurse Sullivan as it was not unusual for him to suddenly go off on some jaunt or other. A subsequent inquest found that Brian Sullivan had committed suicide, and it was only after the discovery of the torso in the River Severn, and police enquiries about missing middle-aged men, that a connection was established between Sullivan and Butt.

Tower Lodge became the scene of an intense police search. Some of Butt's clothing was found there, as was twine very similar to that used to tie bricks to the body parts. Ashes suggested large fires had taken place in the garden and in the living-room grate, where, amongst the ashes, much partly-burned male clothing was discovered. A lot of the garden was dug up in an effort to find evidence, but nothing of real significance was found. The police were sure the torso in the river was that of Captain Butt and, while it was likely that he had been murdered and butchered at Tower Lodge, theories were conjectural and based on fairly scant circumstantial evidence. Rumours were rife, and included suggestions that Butt and Sullivan had been involved in a homosexual affair, that Brian and his mother were involved in an illegal abortion racket, and that the Captain was involved in black magic rites. There was no actual evidence to support these accusations.

The torso was never officially identified as that of Captain Butt and the head has never been found. The jury had little option but to bring in an open verdict on an unknown man. A solution to the Haw Bridge 'torso mystery' remains as elusive as ever, and although Tower Lodge retains an air of mystery for those familiar with the case, it is likely that relatively few people passing by are aware of its grisly past. A local belief that the building is haunted may well be a legacy of the murderous activity thought to have taken place there.

Sightings of UFOs in the skies over the Cheltenham area are not quite as rare as 'torso murders'. Inevitably, though, the credibility of the witnesses is stronger in some cases than others. Police officers usually try to observe situations with a dispassionate and critical eye, so a 1975 incident – in which an officer saw a UFO near a radio mast on top of Cleeve Hill, above Cheltenham – is of particular interest. He had been sent to investigate reports of a stationary light above the mast and, on approaching up the narrow road towards the structure, saw a large, bright UFO hovering in the air nearby.

The officer got out of his vehicle and watched the light for a matter of seconds before it moved silently away and along the contours of a nearby ridge. Then, returning to the police vehicle, he set off in pursuit of the light, which at one point actually crossed the road ahead of him. His instinctive reaction was to flash the car headlights, and at this

Tower Lodge, Leckhampton Hill, Cheltenham.

the UFO shot off at very high speed and disappeared from view. Within moments, the policeman saw a colleague in another police vehicle. This officer corroborated that he, too, had seen the UFO flying across the sky at great speed.

It may be recalled that in 1976 residents in the UK endured an especially hot summer. It was in this year that another police officer reportedly had – not one, but two – extraordinary UFO encounters. In the first experience he was driving towards Cheltenham Police Station to commence duty at 2 p.m. when he heard an external 'clanking' noise. Often this is a warning that the exhaust pipe of one's vehicle has broken free of its housing, but this officer's experience was considerably less mundane. To the left of his car he saw what he described as a '3-pronged UFO, which appeared to have a barbell on the end of one of its arms'. The object, which was moving slowly at low altitude, was the size of a civil airliner. The officer was understandably amazed, and as he watched for some two minutes – having, one assumes, brought his vehicle to a standstill – the barbell appendage seemed to become transparent and in his mind's eye he saw the image of a humanoid figure.

The encounter seems truly fantastic, although the policeman's next experience – just a few months later – is no less extraordinary. On this occasion he observed a 'flying cross', which was the size of a 'jumbo jet' aircraft, in the vicinity of Cheltenham's Hesters Way suburb – a fairly densely populated area. The bizarre UFO, which had a flashing red light at the end of one of its arms, hovered above a church before disappearing from view. Perhaps surprisingly, given the circumstances, there appear to have been no independent witnesses.

No further substantially unusual activity was seen in the skies above Cheltenham for some years. Strange 'bobbing' lights were witnessed late one evening in August 1995, however, with several members of one family seeing an intense pulsating light with a reddish-orange centre moving slowly across the sky. At one point the light suddenly dropped about 100ft, before bobbing back up to its former position. This aerial activity was witnessed by neighbours, too, and a number of Cheltenham residents independently reported seeing similar lights in the area that evening.

Police officers and security guards are quite well placed to see strange lights in the sky, since they are often awake and alert at times when much of the population is asleep in bed. In the early hours of one morning in April 1996 two security guards at Cheltenham's 'secret' Government Communications Headquarters were amazed to see two bright lights fly at very high speed over the base. The witnesses were certain that the lights were not comets.

The most recent account, which dates from July 2005, is perhaps the most convincing – having been reported by a number of people, including a retired police officer who holds a pilot's licence. The incident occurred late one evening, when a series of orange lights was seen above Cheltenham by several people attending a garden party. Additionally, the strange lights were spotted by a coach driver who was returning from London with her passengers. As they stared up in amazement at the lights the driver pulled off the road on the edge of town to enable them to get out and obtain a better view. The retired police officer (who is personally known to the author as a very reliable and level-headed man) and his wife and six friends saw the lights from a house in Cheltenham. He described how at one point the lights appeared to take up the positions of the stars in The Plough, in a way not dissimilar to a scene in the 1977 movie *Close Encounters of the Third Kind*, before drifting apart again. He was quite certain the lights were not those of conventional aircraft and, having held a pilot's licence for more than thirty years, was well aware of the sort of lights one would expect to see.

At around the same time, a man was out running nearby with his wife when they saw the lights stop and hover above them both, before fading and dispersing. The managing director of Gloucestershire Airport advised local newspaper *The Gloucestershire Echo* that 'Lights on aircraft are red, white or green – not orange.'

Now, with a deft leap, we move from UFOs to alien wild beasts. Many thousands of reports of sightings of big cats – usually suggested to be panthers or leopards – have been received in the UK, and Gloucestershire is undoubtedly one of the 'hotspot' areas for such reports. One might well be justified in being alarmed if such creatures were regularly being seen in cities and towns as large as Cheltenham, but evidence of big cat activity in the area is minimal. Whether the woods and fields beyond the roads and houses of Cheltenham town are more inviting to such beasts is a matter for guesswork, but in the mid-1990s a 'large black animal' was seen 'slinking alongside a hedge' in a field to the west of the town. Without any supporting evidence, however, this report is really of curiosity value only.

CHERINGTON

This small village is situated in an area that abounds with relics of the Neolithic period. Long barrows can still be seen at nearby Gatcombe Park, while the famous 'holed' long stone stands in a field between Cherington and Minchinhampton. Less well known, however, is The Devil's Churchyard – a roughly L-shaped enclosure in open fields beside a track on Cherrington Common, to the north of the village. It is said that an ancient stone circle once existed at the site, although no such circle can be seen today.

An interesting legend is told to explain how the place got its name. The owner of Lammas Park in nearby Minchinhampton decided to build a new church, and wishing to strengthen the hold of Christianity in what was a predominantly pagan area ordered the church to be built upon the stone circle. Attempts to construct the building were frustrated, it is said, when each day's work was torn down during the night. This was considered to be the work of the Devil, and when similar destruction occurred on successive occasions it was decided to abandon the project and instead put up the church in Minchinhampton itself. The clergy had the 'unholy' stones removed and taken to Lammas Park.

While some historians have stated their belief that a stone circle probably did once stand on The Devil's Churchyard, others have cast doubt on the notion, suggesting that the 'circle' may have been no more than a natural outcrop of rock. Whatever the reality of

The Lammas Stones, Minchinhampton.

the matter, it is a fact that three of the stones can still be seen today inside the gateway to Lammas House in Minchinhampton.

Another legend connected with the site involves a man who once went nut-picking there. He heard the faint sound of tinkling bells coming from across the fields, and as he stood and listened the sound grew louder and a horse and rider jumped over the nearby hedgerow. In terror, the man saw that the rider was a ghostly figure in black robes. The man turned and ran, not stopping until he reached the High Street at Minchinhampton.

CHIPPING CAMPDEN

The town of Chipping Campden, situated at the northern tip of the North Cotswolds district, is certainly one of the loveliest in Gloucestershire. Indeed, many would consider it one of the most attractive and unspoilt towns in the country. Behind the chocolate-box façade, however, it is steeped in folklore, mystery and superstition – with stories of ghosts and witches forming regular conversation between some of the older inhabitants.

A story that has for many years been known as 'The Campden Wonder' is perhaps the strangest tale to come out of Chipping Campden, having, as it does, elements of murder, mystery, betrayal, wrongful conviction and execution. The known facts are fairly

Chipping Camden Church, from the site of Campden House.

straightforward. On 16 August 1660 William Harrison, aged seventy, a steward to Lady Juliana, Viscountess Campden (then living in the Court House), set out from Chipping Campden to collect rents for her. He did not return that evening, so his wife sent their servant, John Perry, to look for him. Apparently, Perry spent the entire night searching for Harrison, but was unable to find him. When dawn broke and there was still no sign of Harrison or Perry, Edward Harrison, son of the missing man, set out to try and find news of his father. He headed for the village of Charingworth – about three miles east of Chipping Campden – where he knew his father had been intending to collect rents. Edward Harrison met Perry along the way, and together they called at the village of Ebrington, between Charingworth and Chipping Campden. Their enquiries in the village revealed that the missing man had called there to collect rents, so they returned to Chipping Campden.

Good news did not greet them when they got back to the town. During their absence it had become known that a hat, neckband and comb belonging to the missing man had been found among some gorse plants by an old woman at Ebrington. In an ominous indication of foul play, the neckband was blood-stained and the comb appeared to have been hacked about. Most people suspected that William Harrison had been accosted and murdered for the money he was carrying, and suspicion fell on Perry – especially from Harrison's wife, who saw no good reason why Perry had not returned during the night. Called before the magistrates to give an explanation of his actions, Perry gave various stories to account for his master's disappearance. Harrison had indeed been murdered, he said. First of all he claimed the assailant to have been a tinker, then that the deed had been carried out by a servant who had hidden the body in a bean-rick. Nothing was found in the rick, however, and Perry was remanded in custody for a further week. At the end of that week he asked to see the magistrate again, so that the truth could be told. The account he gave caused a sensation.

Perry claimed that his mother and brother had robbed and murdered Harrison. He had played no part in it, other than to tell them where and when he would be passing. In fact, said Perry, he had arrived on the scene to find them in the act of assaulting Harrison, and he had witnessed his brother strangle him. The body was dumped in Campden House's cesspit. John Perry's mother, Joan, and brother, Richard, were immediately arrested and the cesspit was dragged, although no corpse was found, and both Joan and Richard vigorously protested their innocence of the charges. At the next assizes they were brought before Judge Sir Christopher Turner but, as no body had been found, he dismissed the case.

The three were detained for several further months – during which time John Perry persisted in his account – but were up again at the following assizes before Sir Robert Hyde. At this second trial all three pleaded their innocence but, unconvinced, the jury returned a 'guilty' verdict and the Perrys were sentenced to be hanged. They were taken to Broadway Hill, where the deed was done – John was gibbeted, but his mother and brother were buried at the foot of the gallows. There, one might have thought, was where the mystery ended. The three Perrys had died, taking their guilty secret to the grave. What they had done with poor William Harrison and his brutally strangled body might never have come to light.

Something did come to light, however. On 6 August 1662, almost two years after the three executions, William Harrison himself came to light – and not by some mystical séance or in the form of a ghostly apparition. He had an amazing – almost unbelievable – explanation for his disappearance. When returning to Chipping Campden after collecting the rents, he said, he had been set upon by three men on horseback. He resisted, but received a stab-wound and was soon overpowered. He was then taken to Deal in Kent, where he was put in the charge of a mysterious stranger and placed on a boat, which set sail across the high seas. The boat was met by three Turkish ships and Harrison, along with a number of other prisoners, was sold as a slave. He was fortunate to have been purchased by an elderly and kindly physician, who in due course gave him a silver bowl as a reward for his services. The physician died and, using the silver bowl as a bargaining tool, Harrison managed to procure a passage back to England.

Astonishingly, his yarn seems to have been widely believed. Indeed, the whole mysterious episode was suspected to have been the result of a spell cast by Joan Perry, who was considered by many to have been a witch. In more modern times, however, various explanations have been suggested to account for this curious episode, although few stand up to critical analysis. *The Campden Wonder*, edited by Sir George Clark in 1959, offers several theories, one of which is by Lord Maugham, a former Lord Chancellor. In this it is suggested that William Harrison had been embezzling Viscountess Campden's money during the unsettled period between the rule of Cromwell and the throne being taken by King Charles II. It was likely that his dishonesty would have been revealed on the return of law, so he staged a 'murder' and – living on his ill-gotten gains – disappeared. Meanwhile the trial and execution of the Perrys accounted for the loss of money from Viscountess Campden, meaning that he could return when it suited him.

His return did not seem to provide his wife with much cheer. She became depressed and hanged herself, although he lived on as a respected citizen of the town for some years. In recent years, even, this case of injustice has been cited as an example of why capital punishment should never be re-introduced.

Another – slightly less ancient – tale from Chipping Campden concerns a man named Marshal. He is supposed to have been hanged early in the nineteenth century at the point where George Lane meets Catbrook Corner – although what his crime was is not known. Years ago, there used to be a triangular patch of grass with a pile of stones upon it at the junction. These, apparently, were so placed to prevent the dead man from rising out of the ground. It did not work, though, and Marshal's ghost was frequently seen at the location for many years following his execution. This is merely an old folk tale, however, with many years having passed since the ghost was last seen.

Like many places in the Cotswolds and beyond, Chipping Campden has its phantom white ladies. One is said to appear in Dark Coppice on Aston Hill, and another (or possibly the same one) crosses the road at midnight. The white lady at Dover's Hill – a beauty spot with an excellent view over the Vale of Evesham – is probably the most widely known, however, with an accompanying tale of tragedy to explain her presence.

During the time of the Civil War two Chipping Campden families supported different sides during the troubles. A lovely young lady – for they are *all* lovely in such tales – named Beatrice was of a family that supported the Parliamentarian side, while a neighbour, Sir Roger, fought for the Royalists. King Charles I was beheaded in 1649, of course, and when Cromwell assumed power Sir Roger lost his properties to the Parliamentarians. No longer possessing the financial means to live, Sir Roger took to highway robbery, becoming known as 'the Black Knight'. One day, the story goes, he held up a coach on the road to Broadway, little knowing that Beatrice was inside. She did not reveal the Black Knight's identity, however, and – almost inevitable in such tales – the two were soon helplessly in love. They would meet secretly at a gate near the foot of the hill after Beatrice had waved a white silk cloak to let Sir Roger know the way was clear.

The secret meetings were not, however, as secret as the couple believed. Beatrice's two brothers, John and Maurice, came to know of the liaisons and hatched a plan to deal with the Black Knight and his amorous designs upon their sister. First they sent Beatrice to stay with relatives then, going to the gate at the foot of the hill, they waved a white cloak to lure Sir Roger towards them. He saw the cloak and rode unwittingly towards the brothers, but was waylaid and killed by them. Beatrice lost her mind on hearing what had happened, spending the rest of her days in a madhouse. It is said that for many years after the event a white lady apparition – claimed to be the ghost of Beatrice, forlornly waving a white cloak – was occasionally seen near the gate at the foot of the hill.

There are other, lesser-known, stories of ghosts and spectres in and around the town – some are relatively recent, while others are very old. A story concerning Chipping

Dover's Hill, Chipping Campden.

Campden's ghost bear was described in H.J. Massingham's 1938 book *Shepherd's Country*. Apparently a dark-haired foreigner would visit the towns and villages in the North Cotswolds from time to time, bringing with him a bear that would dance while he played the fiddle. During one harsh winter the fiddle-playing foreigner and his performing bear were seen coming down Westington Hill into the town, and, as was usual, the pair went to a house near Heavenly Corner, where they slept together in a shed or out-building.

It soon became known, however, that the foreigner was very ill and, despite the efforts of a local doctor, he died – some gypsies from the Cheltenham area arriving on the scene and taking the bear away. It was never properly determined what became of the animal, but there were two widely-held beliefs – the first account being that it had been shot after becoming savage, while the majority view was that it simply pined away and died.

It was not the last that was heard of the bear, however. Local people described how, during the following winter, they had seen 'a big shambling beast' wandering about Heavenly Corner after dusk. This, it was said, was the ghost of the dancing bear looking for his master.

An interesting account was received some years ago by this author. It concerns the sighting by several people of the ghost of a little girl who, many years ago, may have met with a tragic accident at Robins Cottage in Chipping Campden's Park Road. The earliest report of the sighting came in the first quarter of the twentieth century from a man, then living in the cottage, who claimed that on many occasions he saw the ghost of a little girl. She was invariably waving her arms frantically in the air and, apparently on fire, she would run down the length of the back garden and jump into the stream at its foot.

Generally, however, the man was considered to be more than a little odd. This view was compounded when he was one day discovered digging into a section of the floor inside his home, claiming that he had seen the little girl's ghost descending into the ground. He continued to report seeing the girl, and in an effort to ease the situation exorcisms were conducted on several occasions at the cottage. Even so, most seemed to think the ghost was a figment of the man's imagination.

Little more was heard until some years later a new occupant moved into the cottage, and he too reported seeing an apparition of a little girl in the back garden. Again, nothing more came to light for some considerable time, until two small children staying with the resident of the neighbouring cottage provided a curious account of something they had apparently seen. They told how they had seen a little girl waving her arms in the air, running down the back garden of Robins Cottage and jumping into the stream. The small children – who knew nothing of ghosts and apparitions – said that the girl had long hair and wore a dress that extended below her knees. Her body, they said, seemed to be surrounded by a blue light.

It would be surprising if none of Chipping Campden's hotels and inns had a resident ghost. Perhaps many of them do but, to date, only two reports have been received. The ghost of an elderly former customer has been seen by several people at The Eight Bells Inn, which is the town's oldest hostelry, and at the Cotswold House Hotel in the Square, several reports of a ghost were received in the 1970s. These concerned an apparition described as that of an elderly lady with her hair in long white curls.

According to Anthony Poulton-Smith in his book *Paranormal Cotswolds*, Chipping Campden's Tourist Information Centre in the High Street is the latest place in the town to experience paranormal activity. He describes unexplained events such as 'knocking and shuffling sounds' and 'whispers and hushed voices'. In its former life, and until the later years of the twentieth century, the property was a police station and court, and it has been said that in the 1950s or 1960s an officer on duty alone in the building committed suicide in the cells area.

CIRENCESTER

During the Roman occupation, Cirencester – at that time called Corinium – was Britain's second largest city. Far from that today, of course, it is nevertheless a thriving (and very attractive) market town. The town's first recorded mysterious event may well have its origins in the Roman period.

In 1685 two men digging a gravel pit at Torbarrow Hill, a little to the north of the town, discovered a chamber in the hill. By candlelight they saw that the place they had entered seemed to be some kind of hall, with long tables and benches on each side. Additionally, the chamber contained earthenware urns filled with coins and medals inscribed with Latin text and the heads of Roman emperors. The men found a passage leading into another room, but as they entered they were confronted by the image of a knight, with two embalmed bodies close by. The apparition of the knight struck out towards the men, they said, extinguishing the light and issuing a low moan. Not surprisingly, the men departed as quickly as they could – grabbing a handful of coins as they fled. The roof of the chamber collapsed behind them, burying the ghostly knight.

In due course the men returned to the site of their discovery, only to find that the chamber and its entrance had vanished. Fortunately, however, they still had the coins, which were sold at auction – the incredible way in which they had apparently been found no doubt attracting considerable interest. It is said that the apparition of the knight has been seen at the hill a few times since, although it has been suggested that he may be more of a legionnaire than a knight.

Given the notable history of the place, it is somewhat surprising that there are not far more legends and accounts of mysterious events associated with Cirencester. There are vague stories of a 'grey lady' phantom that has been seen in the splendid Church of St James, but the only relatively substantial accounts are those that are associated with two of the town's inns – The Black Horse and The King's Head. A ghost at The Black Horse became the subject of press attention when it appeared to the licensee's niece staying at the inn in 1933. She was awakened at midnight to find her room lit by a strange light, and she saw the apparition of an evil-looking old woman float across the room and through a wall. It was subsequently found that some panelling in the room concealed a window, and etched upon one of the panes was the name 'James'. The spectre was thereafter seen on numerous occasions and by various individuals, becoming such a nuisance that a medium was summoned to try and solve the problem. After visiting, and perambulating around the rooms of the inn, the medium explained that the ghost of the old woman was earthbound, having done some harm to an old man in one of the rooms. The medium gave instructions on how to lay the ghost: three white flowers were to be laid in the room at 3 p.m. on the third day of the month. The procedure was carried out; apparently being effective, for no further trouble was reported. There has, however, been some further activity in more-recent decades – although this has been nowhere near as troublesome as the initial haunting. A landlord in the early 1970s reported a number of strange occurrences, then, in 1999, guests reported seeing an oddly dressed old woman upstairs and the apparition has been seen very occasionally at other times, too.

The ghosts at The King's Head may well be connected with historical situations. In the basement of the building is a crypt area known as The Monks' Retreat, with a blocked-up passage that once led beneath the Market Place outside to the cellars of the Abbey Penitentiary opposite. Night porters and other staff members have on several occasions seen apparitional figures of monks in the building, clothed in traditional habit and with the cowl pulled up over the face.

In 1688, when William of Orange landed in England, a skirmish took place outside The King's Head in Cirencester when Lord Lovelace was on his way with his men to join forces with the new king. Supporters of the Stuarts shot a member of Lovelace's party – one Bulstrode Whitelock – and he was taken into the building, where he died of his wounds. The room to which he was taken has been the scene of various paranormal occurrences, and one night porter was terrified when a ghostly Cavalier shot a pistol in his direction! No bullet actually struck anything, but the employee was so shaken that he left the hotel, never to return. Furthermore, a 1995 report in *The Gloucestershire Echo* described how a Dutch tourist 'fled in terror' from the hotel after waking in the night, feeling very cold, and seeing the figure of a Cavalier standing near his bed.

As well as being home to ghostly monks and gun-toting apparitions, The King's Head has had more than its fair share of other inexplicable events, including poltergeist activity, doors opening and closing of their own accord, footsteps pacing across empty rooms, icy draughts – and even a dancing fireball in the ballroom. This building certainly seems fertile ground for those wishing to experience paranormal activity.

The most recent mysterious activities in Cirencester, however, concern not ghosts, but alien big cats. In recent years people have made several reports of seeing large, unidentified animals on the edge of the town, with a local newspaper reporting in 2005 that they had received dozens of calls from residents claiming to have seen a puma-like beast in the Cirencester area. Indeed, that year seemed particularly busy in terms of big cat sightings. Credence was given to the idea of a big cat prowling around the area when in June the chief executive of Cotswolds District Council reported seeing a jet black panther-like beast on playing fields near his home at Stratton, on the edge of Cirencester. About the size of a Labrador dog, the animal measured about 2ft in height and 4ft in length, with a thick tail. The witness said that it was definitely not a domestic cat or dog.

Later that same year, local newspaper *The Wiltshire and Gloucestershire Standard* used its front page to feature a CCTV picture of a large black feline taken near Cirencester Hospital. Although a rather grainy picture, it does appear to show a large black cat at least 4½ft in length walking next to a zebra crossing.

Big Cat caught on Cirencester Hospital CCTV.
(Photograph courtesy of Gloucestershire Health Authority)

All was relatively quiet for some time after this appearance, although stories of a big cat being seen in the Chesterton area of Cirencester continued to surface from time to time. Then, in February 2010, the *Wilts and Gloucestershire Standard* reported that a couple driving in Cranhams Lane, Chesterton in the early hours of the morning had spotted a big cat. Described as 'definitely feline', the animal was said to be black-coloured, bigger than a Labrador dog and with a long tail. Big cat expert Frank Tunbridge was quoted as saying that he often heard of sightings in the Chesterton area.

CLEARWELL

The striking neo-Gothic Clearwell Castle has a long history and, though the present building is a restoration of a house built in the 1720s, it is claimed that it has been a home since Roman times. There is a story that the apparition of a beautiful lady in a red silk dress has been seen in a window seat. Especially notable, apparently, is her exquisite perfume, which sometimes pervades the entire building.

In the early 1970s quintessential heavy metal band Black Sabbath were for a time based in the castle during a writing session for an album that would become *Sabbath Bloody Sabbath*. Tony Iommi, their legendary lead guitarist, has described how he and another band member saw an apparitional cloaked figure in the castle dungeons. They saw the figure as they were setting up their equipment and followed it into a room, only to find there was no one there when they entered. When they told the castle's owners about the incident, they were advised that it was the resident ghost.

Also in the village is a natural cave system that was filled with deposits of iron ore millions of years ago. The first attempts at mining the iron minerals deposited around the walls and caverns were made by Iron Age man, although it was the Romans who really developed the mining industry. The mining continued for many more centuries, the last iron ore being raised commercially in 1945. Eight large caverns are today open to the public.

The ghost of an old miner is said to haunt the Ham mine at Clearwell. A television crew filming deep in the caverns in the 1960s were frustrated when an old man wandered across the set. He ignored warning shouts, and a crew-member approached him to offer appropriate advice. Apparently oblivious, however, the old man walked straight through the crew-member. A group of local men went down into the mine one evening, hoping to see the ghost for themselves. However, their enthusiasm rapidly evaporated when they actually did see something unusual. An orange glow was seen in the back of the cave, and a shadowy figure carrying a light passed across the cavern about twenty yards distant. This was followed by a chinking sound, as though the figure was chipping at the rock. This was seen and heard by several people in the group – one even having seen a pick axe in the figure's hand.

A commercial park named the Baden Watkins car park, with an old horse-drawn tram-road running along the back of it, is situated near the village. This is said to be haunted by the spirit of a bad-tempered miner who was killed by a truck on the tram line. A lorry driver who parked in the car park one night was pushed violently on the shoulder when he got out of his truck, and another man found the body of his car marked by a line of footprints that led from the front and over the roof to the back of the vehicle. The popular explanation, apparently, was that he had simply parked his car in the line of the ghostly miner's nightly stroll.

Clearwell Castle.

COALEY

Not too much seems mysterious about this little village just below the Cotswold edge. Many years ago people swore that Coaley churchyard harboured a thin, misty white phantom that was shaped like a pillar and stood 4ft above the ground, but this fearsome entity turned out in fact to be gas rising from some rotten wood.

There is, however, thought to be a ghost at The Fox and Hounds – the village's welcoming community pub. It seems that a former landlady shows a reluctance to move on, and this middle-aged lady's apparition has been seen upstairs in the private quarters as well as in the bar area. Witnesses have been able to recognise her as a former licensee because she is included in a photograph on one of the pub walls.

COLEFORD

The last town in the Forest of Dean before the border between England and Wales, Coleford was originally a mining centre, and at nearby Milkwall, a little to the south of the town, the evocative remains of early opencast iron workings may be seen at Puzzle Wood. These ancient mines – known locally as 'scowles' – were worked thousands of years ago by Iron Age man and the Romans, the remains today presenting an interesting and mysterious series of paths through overhanging creepers and moss-covered rocks. The town's mining past has long-since given way to alternative industry, and Coleford is nowadays a popular centre for those wishing to explore the forest and nearby Wye Valley.

There are several accounts of ghosts and incidences of haunting in Coleford. The Angel Hotel in the town's Market Place dates from the seventeenth century and is said to be haunted by the ghost of a Cavalier, although when this apparition was last seen is not known. In the 1990s a spectral carriage and four horses was seen careering rapidly along the Bream Road, the vision apparently having caused 'many a car to crash'. This and several other accounts are described in *Ghosts of the Forest of Dean*, an interesting little booklet by Sue Law.

The Coombs at Coleford's Sparrow Hill is today a residential care home for the elderly, but was built in the nineteenth century by local landowner and magistrate Isaiah Trotter, who lived there for many years. It is believed that a female member of the Trotter family hanged herself in the stables many years ago, and it is said that her restless spirit still haunts the house and grounds. The apparition of a lady in a long grey dress has been seen, and inexplicable noises have included the rattling of doors, ghostly footsteps, and the sounds of voices and laughter. On one memorable occasion a member of staff at the home heard a 'bloodcurdling scream' that 'seemed to fill the whole house'. Fortunately for staff and residents, the ghostly activity has in recent years become less frequent.

Coleford's police station, too, seems to be the focus for some minor paranormal activity, and officers on duty there have reported hearing the inexplicable sounds of footsteps and the slamming of doors. The station's interview room, apparently, has a particularly unpleasant 'feeling' to it – not least, probably, for suspected criminals under interrogation – and a 'ghostly motorbike' has been heard to pull up at the entrance to the building. Regrettably, no officer has actually seen the phantom bike, nor been able to obtain its registration number.

In common with many places in the Forest of Dean, Coleford possibly has a big cat that roams the area. In 1997 a motorist travelling near the town in the early hours of the morning saw a black animal jump from the road and into some undergrowth by the roadside. The animal was described as '…definitely not a deer. It had a long tail … It was cat-like and black all over…'

COMPTON ABDALE

The Puesdown Inn at Compton Abdale is not situated in the village itself, but stands beside the busy A40 road from Cheltenham to Oxford. A very old coaching inn, thought to date from the thirteenth century, the place has long been regarded as the site of incidences of haunting and supernatural activity, with more than one person reporting seeing a coach and four horses crossing the main road outside the inn.

The inn itself has been plagued by all sorts of odd activities, from ghostly footsteps to rapping and shuffling sounds. One licensee even claimed to have seen a phantom coach and horses, accompanied by the sound of jingling harnesses, draw into the inn's yard one night. There has been poltergeist activity, too, with televisions and other appliances behaving strangely, and one couple in bed at night were startled by some unseen entity pulling at their bedclothes. The most recent activity took place in 2004 when waitresses serving glasses of champagne from a tray to a wedding party were unnerved when the tray tipped up of its own accord, the glasses all breaking on the floor. This happened three times in succession.

The section of road outside was at one time infamous as the haunt of highwaymen. One tradition has it that a highwayman was shot nearby, and made his way to the inn, banging desperately at the door to be let in. He was taken inside and died soon after. Rapping sounds still heard from time to time are believed to be caused by the ghost of the highwayman.

COOMBE HILL

This part of Gloucestershire has been – if legend is to be believed – a favourite haunt of dragons and sea serpents. An illustration of the Sea Serpent of Coombe Hill, drawn in 1904, appeared in the *Cheltenham Chronicle and Gloucestershire Graphic* of that year. Many years ago, it was claimed, a large and hideous sea monster made its way up the River Severn and settled on the riverbank.

It seems that the creature was initially content to feed on sheep and poultry, but then it began to prey upon children and milkmaids. The villagers of Coombe Hill found their lives constantly blighted by the serpent until one day a local fellow named Tom Smith hatched a cunning plan to overcome it. He began leaving food out for the serpent and, by means of this ploy, gained its trust and confidence. One day, so the legend goes, Smith was feeding the monster by hand and seized the opportunity to smash an axe upon its head. Such was the strength of the blow that the serpent was killed instantly, and Smith received a generous reward of limitless beer at the village pub.

It will be seen that the nearby villages of Deerhurst and Tredington had their own monsters to contend with, and in the case of Tredington a fossilised 'fish-lizard' may be seen in the church to this day.

CRANHAM

There are several folklore tales based in and around this village. Various apparitions are supposed to have been seen in the woodland around the village, and the ghostly form of an elderly woman is said to have several times been seen roaming the woods. As recently as the early years of the twenty-first century an apparitional coach and horses has been seen on the Buckholt Road.

A useful website *Strange Stroud and District* makes mention of a tale with 'questionable origins', in which a group of friends walking around the village after dark found themselves strolling along a track. Suddenly, two of the group fell into a hole but were extricated, with some difficulty. Adjacent to the hole, apparently, was a cottage with large iron gates – behind which the hazy silhouette of a figure was seen staring at the group and their predicament. The group shouted for help, but none was forthcoming, and when they looked again at the figure it had completely vanished. This does seem the kind of account that one might easily imagine to have been fuelled by scrumpy cider or some form of herbal substance.

Behind the Royal William pub stands the remains of an ancient burial mound, said to be the last resting place of a British chieftain named Eddel. According to tradition, he haunts the area still, and his ghost has been seen near the burial mound. This is very much a folk tale, however, and there seems to be no record of any sighting within living memory.

DEERHURST

A few miles to the south of Tewkesbury the little village of Deerhurst can be found in fields just beyond the banks of the River Severn. At first glance the place looks pretty enough – with its timber-framed cottages and air of quiet prosperity – but seems unexceptional. Its Anglo-Saxon church, however, is one of the oldest in England and is full of carvings of mythical serpents and dragons. Two unrecognisable animal heads project from the west wall of the church and are believed to have been the inspiration for the tradition of a local dragon or serpent. Sir Robert Atkyns, in his 1712 work *The Ancient and Present State of Gloucestershire*, describes the legend thus:

There lived in the vicinity of deerhurst a serpent of prodigious bigness. It poisoned the people and the cattle and ravaged the land. The king issued a decree to the effect that whoever could rid the land of this menace would receive a grant of land, the estate of walton hill. The task was undertaken by one john smith, a labouring man. He went to the serpents favourite resting place where he found the beast asleep in the sun. With a mighty blow of his axe he cleaved the head of the serpent from its body, so ridding the land of the beast forever.

In the late eighteenth century a local man claimed to have the axe in his possession, although it is not known what has become of it since. As recently as the late nineteenth century, apparently, villagers continued to regard the tale as a true account. It is curious that the serpent-slayer's name was John Smith, while the serpent-slayer at nearby Coombe Hill was Tom Smith – are they really one and the same?

Less fearsome than the serpent, but unlikely to be a welcome presence, is the belligerent ghost that is believed to haunt the churchyard. This phantom, said to be that of a tall man in rustic clothing, appears angry and shakes his fist at onlookers. Unusually, it is claimed that he has even given voice to his emotions – yelling at intruders.

DRAYCOTT

Beast Head at the exterior of Deerhurst Church.

There are no records of ghosts or phantoms appearing in the small village of Draycott, and in general there seems little that could be called genuinely mysterious – unless, of course, one relates a tale described to this author some years ago.

A man at that time locally resident was walking through the village one clear, moonlit evening in 1961 when a large flying saucer – described as 'larger than a double decker bus' – appeared from the direction of Blockley and stopped to hover nearby. The UFO resembled a huge spinning top and had white lights on its upper side and purple lights on its underside, and although it made very little noise its appearance was accompanied by a slight whistling sound.

It seemed to the witness that the craft was visible for several minutes but, unwilling to stay in the vicinity, he ran to his home nearby. The door was opened by the man's wife, who saw the object fly away at very high speed towards Moreton-in-Marsh. A similar, unconnected, report of a UFO sighting at around the same time was subsequently received from a resident of that town, lending the original story somewhat greater credibility than might otherwise have been the case.

DUMBLETON

The twelfth-century church of St Peter merits inclusion as a place of some mystery because the tympanum of the north doorway bears a particularly unusual foliate head, or 'green man', carving. This pagan image of a man's head has the ears of an ass, and three pieces of foliage issuing from its mouth, and although the green man is often thought to represent fertility and regeneration this particular carving is sometimes suggested to be a representation of the Devil.

The churchyard, too, is not without an air of mystery, for it is claimed to be the haunt of a spectral white lady who walks there after darkness has fallen. Roy Palmer, in his book *Folklore of Gloucestershire*, mentions that a spectral grey lady has been seen on the stairs at Dumbleton Hall.

DUNTISBOURNE ABBOTS

This neat little village in the valley of the Dunt stream takes its name from the abbots of Gloucester, to whom it once belonged. A quiet place, it is the setting for another classic

'Green Man' at Dumbleton Church.

'white lady' apparition. Roy Palmer, in his book *Folklore of Gloucestershire*, describes how she appears by a holly tree in the wall of the Old Mill House before driving a coach and horses across a meadow opposite.

The likelihood is that this is a very old tale; although Rupert Matthews in his 2006 book *Haunted Gloucestershire* states that she is seen 'quite often', so perhaps the ghost is still active.

DURSLEY

A traditional tale concerning a mysterious inn said to have existed on the Downly Hill area above Dursley has been described in various books and publications. A very useful book, *The Folklore of the Cotswolds* by Katharine M. Briggs, gives a thorough account of the story, the author stating that the person who related it to her first heard of it in 1966 – although it is probably much older than that.

In essence, the story describes how a man was riding across the wolds to Stroud one dark night when he became caught in a blizzard. He lost sight of the road and despaired of finding shelter, but then suddenly spotted the lights of an inn ahead. He made his way to the inn and was welcomed by a servant in green livery who showed him to a comfortable bedroom, where there was a roaring fire and a meal set in front of it. Even the man's horse was very well cared for, being looked after by a groom who fed the animal with oats and sweet hay. The man enjoyed a good night's sleep, waking to find the fire made up and bread, ale and cheese on the table. He ate his meal, but when he came to depart could not find anyone to pay, so left two gold guineas on the table.

When he got to Stroud the man told his friends about the unusually hospitable inn above Dursley. They were surprised at the account, saying that no such inn existed at the place described; however, they agreed to accompany their friend so that they could see the inn for themselves. The man retraced his steps, taking his friends to the exact spot where he had seen the inn. But there was no building there. All that could be seen were two golden guineas lying in the snow.

'I'm told they come out on stormy nights,' said the wife of one of the man's friends, 'and they never take payment. They never stay after cockcrow. It's lucky you went early or you'd have waked in the snow.'

Folklorists Jennifer Westwood and Jacqueline Simpson in their 2005 book *The Lore of the Land* observe that elements of the story suggest fairies, not ghosts, were responsible for the kindness shown to the man and his horse.

The Old Bell Hotel in Dursley's Long Street, however, seems to be home to ghosts rather than fairies. The building has long been reputed as the focal point for a variety of apparitions and poltergeists, and there are stories of tunnels leading from the cellar, and underneath the road to the nearby church. One of the rooms at the inn was once used as an assize court, apparently, where various individuals were no doubt sent to the gallows. Two of the hotel's ghosts are said to be the tortured souls of innocent men who were hanged. The ghost of a chambermaid named Mabel – said to have hanged herself in one of the rooms – is another regular at the inn, and yet another of the Old Bell's ghosts is said to be that of an old man who was locked up to die in solitary confinement after contracting an infectious disease. Incredibly, even more ghosts have supposedly been seen, with one observer claiming to have seen the apparition of a woman in a red and white striped apron in the main bar, and other reports describing the sighting of a little girl's ghost, and a man in top hat and tails descending the stairs.

There have been other strange occurrences at the Old Bell Hotel. Apparently, one guest was awoken by a booming voice that announced it was eight o'clock, when it was actually the middle of the night, and chairs, tables and cutlery have been mysteriously rearranged in the dining area. In the 1970s one landlord heard the hotel's call bell ringing when unconnected, and as recently as 2006 ghost hunters staying in an upstairs room heard a mysterious bell sound. Some guests staying in the room in which Mabel purportedly hanged herself found their clothes – discarded on the floor when they retired to bed – to have been mysteriously tidied during the night. Was this an activity of Mabel, the ghostly chambermaid? Certainly this old building has much to interest folklorists and students of the paranormal – as well as those who simply enjoy a good story.

An area of Dursley known as The Ridge has a reputation locally as a place that was at one time haunted by the ghost of a murdered woman. The existing building at The Ridge was constructed in the 1960s on the site of an earlier house that had been empty for some years and had become ruinous. During construction work, says Anthony Poulton-Smith in his 2009 book *Paranormal Cotswolds*, builders sensed a 'distinctly malevolent presence' and at one point were gathered in discussion beneath an arch when a potentially fatal incident occurred, adding fuel to the place's unhappy reputation. As the builders stepped away, apparently, the large and heavy keystone dropped onto the ground where they had been standing.

It is said that the occupants of the original house found it necessary to leave the place after they found their lives blighted by the regular attentions of a ghostly lady in white. This lady,

The Old Bell Hotel, Dursley.

apparently, was known to them as a family ancestor who had been murdered in horrific circumstances, and the family would regularly hear her piercing screams filling the house as the dreadful act was replayed again and again. Even after the family had moved out and the house was empty, passers-by in the 1920s heard the playing of a piano from within the deserted building – although there was no piano there, nor anyone to play it. The ghostly reputation grew, of course, and more stories came to light. Unexplained lights were seen flashing in trees outside the house, and decades later an ominous-looking dark figure was seen lurking near the door of the coach house. As far as is known, however, these mysterious events are of their time only, with no known incidences of haunting in recent years.

There are a couple of further stories of minor apparitional and poltergeist activity at unspecified locations in Dursley, and in 1998 a local resident was driving his car late one night on the A38 road from Dursley towards Berkeley when he pulled over to watch what seemed to be a spacecraft hovering 200ft above the ground. He was with his daughter, who had just finished performing waitress duties in the town, when they saw the craft, which was about 20ft long and had four or five white lights along its side, with red and green lights above. The witness was quite certain the craft was not a helicopter.

DYMOCK

A quiet village in the north-west of Gloucestershire, Dymock stands on the site of a substantial Roman settlement – believed by some to be the 'lost' town of *Macatonium*. There is not very much about the place that is truly mysterious, although its church has an interesting thirteenth or fourteenth century stone coffin lid, the origin of which is something of a mystery.

In common with much of England, many of the local inhabitants no doubt once believed in witches and the power of curses. There was actually an infamous Dymock curse that was levelled in the seventeenth century upon an unfortunate woman named Sarah Ellis. An inscribed lead plaque came to light in 1892 (now kept in Gloucester Folk Museum), which bears symbols representing the good and evil influences of the moon, the mystic number 369, and the names of various demons – who are implored to 'make this person to Banish away from this place…' The name at the head of the inscription is 'haraS sillE' (Sarah Ellis backwards). The curse worked, if local tradition is to be believed, for Sarah Ellis is supposed to have committed suicide as a result.

This area is close to the Forest of Dean – reputed haunt of big cats – so it does not require a huge leap of faith to imagine that such beasts may occasionally wander in the vicinity of Dymock. A woman who spotted a panther-like creature near the village in 1994 gave a vivid description: '…I saw this black animal walking down the road towards me. I had a very full view. It was about as high as a sheep but it had the swaggering roll of a cat. It turned totally sideways and I was amazed to see a very long tail which touched the ground and curled up at the end for about 9in. It was a muscley sort of animal, pitch black with a small head and this massive tail. I was watching it for a couple of minutes as it came towards me then it jumped ten or twelve feet up the bank and disappeared.' Even allowing for the possibility of some exaggeration, this description certainly seems to suggest an animal rather more substantial than a household cat.

EBRINGTON

This lovely village of thatched cottages and narrow lanes is well known in the North Cotswolds for once being home to simpletons and half-wits – the famed 'Yubberton Yawnies' – and there are many amusing stories about their moronic exploits. How many of the tales have any basis in truth is really a matter for conjecture and certainly there is no evidence that the present-day population suffers any intellectual deficit. Among the tales is a claim that the Yawnies became jealous of the splendid church tower at neighbouring Chipping Campden, so determined they would encourage the growth of their own church tower by spreading muck around its base. As the muck settled, the Yawnies saw a mark an inch up the wall and swore the tower had grown. A well-known local rhyme describes the event thus:

> The Yubberton Yawnies be so wise
> They mucked the tower to make it rise.
> And when the muck began to sink
> They swore the tower had grown an inch.

There is a tale, too, of how they constructed a roof over a pond in the village so that the ducks might stay dry when it rained; they are supposed to have caged a cuckoo in an orchard so that summer might never leave the village; one Yawnie spent hours sowing seed by hand, but failed to open the shutter of the seed-drill, explaining that this would prevent crows from picking up the seeds; one moonlit night some Yawnies were seen trying to rake out the 'big round cheese' they could see in a pond; once a Yawnie, on being asked where he was going, replied, 'To the place where they boiled a donkey to get his harness off.' On one occasion a Yawnie sat a pig on a wall so that it could 'watch the band march by'. There are no doubt other yarns about the Yubberton Yawnies, and Roy Palmer, in his book *Folklore of Gloucestershire*, describes a number of equally comical stories relating to other villages in the area. Indeed, it seems that some of the stories and locations may have become inter-changeable.

Ebrington is not without ghost stories either. Ernest Belcher's privately printed book *Rambles Among the Cotswolds* describes how one morning in 1780 a farmer was walking across his land near the village when a dense fog fell. He became aware of something close by and suddenly saw an 'old-fashioned sombre-looking coach drawn by six dark horses', speed past and over the brow of the steepest part of the hill. When he ran to the edge of the hill, however, the farmer could see nothing. Rarely mentioned nowadays, this account was originally known locally as the legend of the 'night coach'.

Somewhat more recently, a family living on the Springfield development in the village occasionally saw the apparition of an elderly lady seated in a chair in the house. This occurred over a period of several years, but the ghost has not been seen for some time.

EDGE

Only two folklore accounts based on this small village are known. There is a tradition that the sound of ghostly scything is occasionally heard in fields on Hanging Hill – the result, apparently, of a farmhand who had boasted that he could mow the field in a single day, and who, on failing to achieve his boast, hanged himself.

The second account concerns the sighting of an apparition in the late 1990s. A couple driving on the A4173 approached the edge of the village when they were startled by the sudden appearance of a young girl near the sign. The girl's image then dematerialised as suddenly as it had appeared.

ELKSTONE

The fourteenth-century church at Elkstone has various carvings of grotesques and mythical creatures, with a serpent's head at the south doorway and a centaur around the roofline.

A ghostly white coach and four horses was seen to cross the A417 near The Highwayman Inn by a man driving on the road at dusk one evening in the early 1970s. The inn itself is supposed to have a resident ghost.

EVENLODE

In the 1980s it was reported that several apparitions had been seen at a house named Two Stones, close to the church at Evenlode. Thought to have once been a priest's house, and certainly once a rectory, it seems to be home to a monk, as well as other apparitional figures. The monk, in traditional habit with a cowl, was seen seated at a desk in a downstairs room, and on another occasion in one of the bedrooms. Other witnesses have reported seeing the figure of a lady holding a candle in an upstairs bedroom, and children dancing on the stairs. The lady has been described as elderly and frail, and wearing a bonnet and shawl. A traditional belief is that her son went to fight in the First World War, but never came home, and that the lady – who died during his absence – remains at the house to await his return. Finally, as it became clear that the house was a focal point for paranormal phenomena, it was decided to hold a séance – at which it was concluded that the spirit of a little boy was in the house.

Surprisingly for such a small village, Evenlode has three separate UFO-related stories centred upon it. In the summer of 1960 a local farmer was astonished when two mysterious circles appeared in one of his fields at Poplars Farm, close to the boundary between Gloucestershire and Oxfordshire. The circles were imprinted on green turf – rather than shaped in corn, as is the case with recent crop circles – and were one inside the other, and apparently as accurate as if drawn geometrically. The inner circle

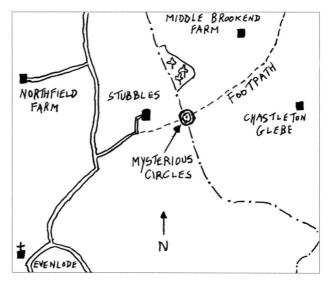

Map showing locaton of two mysterious circles that appeared in a field near Evenlode in 1960.

(16ft across) was more indented than the outer (23ft across) and the turf on the circular lines was slightly discoloured, perhaps as a result of heat.

News of the circles soon spread and numerous local people went to see them, and as the circles were not near any road or habitation no satisfactory explanation was found. A report appeared in local newspaper *The Evesham Journal* in which the reporter, David Day, felt that the circles could only have been made by a large round object pressing hard against the ground. He added that if there were such things as flying saucers, this was exactly the sort of impression one would expect them to make on landing.

The appearance of the circles caused some of Evenlode's residents to recall a previous incident that was not greatly dissimilar. Children attending the village school in the late 1950s were one morning surprised to find that, during the night, three circles had appeared on grass at the back of the school. The circles were 2–3ft in diameter, the circular lines being about 3in in thickness, with whatever had caused them having scorched the peculiar markings onto the grass. The three circles were in a triangular formation – almost as though a very large tripod had been standing on the ground. The school's teacher, baffled by the incident, reported the matter and, it is said, scientists and government officials attended from London and examined the ground. No explanation was ever offered, however.

The third UFO-related account concerns the sighting of a UFO in the night sky in 1966. A man aged eighteen was in Evenlode village when he saw the object, which at first was some distance away above Stow-on-the-Wold. He described the UFO as of tear-drop or pear-drop shape, with a white misted glass appearance and no visible detail. The witness watched the object perform rapid 'figures of eight' movements in the night sky for around twenty minutes before it came towards Evenlode, descending very low as it neared the church. The object made no noise but was, apparently, 'the size of two houses'. The young man became very alarmed when he saw the close proximity of the UFO and, running away, did not see the object again.

Fairford

Prominent in this attractive town on the River Coln is the magnificent St Mary's Church, rebuilt by wealthy wool merchant John Tame in the last thirty years of the fifteenth century. There are depictions of a number of mythical creatures in the building, with external sculptures including a dragon, a wyvern (a two-legged, winged creature with the head of a dragon and the tail of a snake) and a griffin (a winged monster with the head of an eagle and the body of a lion). The church's stained glass is particularly notable, with a Last Judgement window illustrating a hideous two-headed Devil figure, and additionally the building has a set of misericords (ledges beneath tip-up seats, affording support while clergy stood through long services) that bear interesting carvings made around 1520, including a 'green man' and a couple of wyverns.

As with many towns and villages in the district, Fairford has a number of inns and public houses – several of which are believed to be haunted. The Railway Inn, on the Lechlade Road, has been the scene of various minor poltergeist incidents that are all blamed on the ghostly presence of a former landlady, 'Ma Jones', and The Marlborough Arms on the Cirencester Road, too, has seen occasional odd occurrences – such as glasses inexplicably flying off shelves. However, it is probably The Eight Bells Inn near the London Road that has seen more paranormal activity than any other public house in the town. There is a history of fleetingly-seen apparitions and minor poltergeist occurrences, and photographs taken in the bar area have revealed the presence of strange 'orbs' in the air. Investigations of the ghostly occurrences have taken place, with researchers apparently finding evidence of much paranormal activity, although staff and customers have been pleased to find that the presence seems benign.

Devil Figure, Last Judgement Window, Fairford Church.

FLAXLEY

The little village of Flaxley today seems not much more than a handful of pretty cottages with a modern church, although a great moated house, Flaxley Abbey, is nearby. The Cistercian abbey was founded about 1151 by Roger, Earl of Hereford, allegedly on the spot where his father was killed on Christmas Eve 1143, whilst hunting in the Forest of Dean. Following the Dissolution in 1539, the abbey was granted to Sir William Kingston, Constable of the Tower of London, whose main achievement seems to have been the overseeing of Anne Boleyn's execution earlier that year. The overseeing of executions appears to have been a peculiarly sinister vocation for the Kingstons – Sir William's son, Anthony, carried out the execution of Bishop Hooper, burned at the stake at Gloucester in 1555.

At the time of the Dissolution the monk charged with the running of the abbey was one Brother Wulfram, who had been at the abbey for some seventy years. According to tradition, he refused to give up his vows, moving into the cellars of the abandoned and semi-ruined abbey. He died soon afterwards and was buried in the old abbey graveyard, his phantom still occasionally being seen in the vicinity. A useful little booklet *True Ghost Stories of the Forest of Dean* by Dena Bryant-Duncan describes how Wulfram slept in the day then went out at night to gather food, adding that 'several people over the years have seen his bent, grey hooded figure, stooping here and there to pick something'.

Apparently there is another ghost in the area. Rupert Matthews in his book *Haunted Gloucestershire* explains how the sound of a ghostly fiddle is sometimes heard in the area

Flaxley Abbey.

south of the village. Tradition has it that a secret tunnel runs from the old abbey towards the River Severn and that, years ago, the entrance was discovered by some young men. They followed the tunnel, it is said, and they were led by one of their number who played a fiddle so that they might follow the sound. Strangely, the fiddle-player apparently elected to forge ahead alone and almost inevitably the sound abruptly stopped after a while, leaving the explorers in silence. Their lamps suddenly went out, too, so they fled back to the surface, leaving their friend to his fate!

FRAMPTON-ON-SEVERN

Situated near the eastern banks of the magnificent River Severn, the village of Frampton-on-Severn is notable for possessing one of the longest greens in England and for being the birthplace of Henry II's mistress, Fair Rosamund. There have been several reports of ghostly activity in the village although, unfortunately, Rosamund has not made an appearance. Visitors to Frampton Court, a splendid eighteenth-century house in its own park on the east of the green, have encountered the apparition of an elderly lady on the entrance hall stairs, while one former resident of the house heard the sound of heavy footsteps at the rear of the building.

The seventeenth-century timber-framed De Lacy Cottage gained a local reputation as a haunted house in the 1980s when the occupant, Beatrice Phillips, claimed to have seen at

De Lacy Cottage, Frampton-on-Severn.

least five separate apparitions there. A sickly-looking woman was once seen standing near a fireplace in the sitting room, and a small white dog was regularly seen about the house. Other ghostly apparitions seemed to be of historical nature – a woman in Puritan costume was seen in the garden, and on a separate occasion a Roman soldier with helmet and shield strode purposefully across the land there. Perhaps the most interesting sighting was of a group of people in blue and red costumes seen passing the cottage. That same day, the *Gloucester Citizen* newspaper reported the date as the anniversary of the mustering of 'The Frampton Regulars' – a militia formed to repel Napoleon's forces, were they to invade the country. It seems that the witness to all these apparitions was a highly perceptive individual with extra-sensory powers. An alternative view might be that her 'sightings' happened to relate to historical events in the village that she may or may not have known of.

FRANCE LYNCH

Only one account of mysterious activity comes from this hillside village of narrow lanes and steep gradients. The very pleasant village pub, The King's Head, has a poltergeist that has been considered responsible for turning off the gas supply in the cellar, as well as causing the inexplicable movement of a heavy chest. Other peculiar occurrences have taken place, although the ghost does not seem malevolent or particularly troublesome.

The source of this paranormal activity is really a matter for conjecture. There is a tradition, however, that many years ago someone was killed in a bar-room brawl in the building. It could be that the victim's restless spirit accounts for the strange occurrences.

FROCESTER

There are two accounts of mysterious activity from Frocester, and although neither includes any recent sighting or paranormal experience they are considered worthy of inclusion as part of the area's rich folklore heritage.

The first account concerns that hardy perennial, the 'phantom stagecoach'. A tragic stagecoach accident is supposed to have occurred on Frocester Hill many years ago, and there is a tradition that ghostly re-enactments of the accident are said to have been seen. Quite how long ago this sighting occurred is a matter for guesswork – certainly there is no record of any recent sighting – but the account must have been locally well known, for the story has lived on into the twenty-first century.

The second account, too, is quite old. Some bell-ringers from the nearby village of Coaley apparently decided to steal a bell from Frocester. They entered the church late one night, and with much difficulty lowered one of the bells. Before leaving, however, they paused for a smoke in the churchyard. When they returned to the church they found a little old lady clad in a grey cloak sitting on the bell. The old lady ignored the aspiring thieves, and no matter how hard they tried they could not move the bell. Finally they panicked and ran away, with the bell being found next morning and returned to its rightful place. The explanation provided for the strange event was that a local woman had once given jewellery to be cast into the bell, vowing that her spirit would protect it. Apparently, one of Frocester's bells was once found halfway down the tower stairs.

It is said that the grey lady is still seen in the churchyard from time to time. Her figure stands there in the evening, apparently, keeping watch over her precious bell.

GLOUCESTER

The imposing cathedral at Gloucester, with its fifteenth-century tower topped by four delicate pinnacles, is an imposing landmark for miles around and is the source of several of the city's mysterious accounts. Legend claims it has a secret tunnel that leads to the fourteenth-century New Inn at Northgate Street, while another story has it that a subterranean passage leads from the cathedral to nearby Llanthony Abbey. Whether either tunnel actually exists, however, is a matter of some doubt – until, of course, an enterprising explorer discovers some tangible evidence.

The cathedral building itself houses a variety of curious and mysterious features. There are several examples of that enigmatic pagan symbol known as the 'green man'; the Lady

Gloucester Cathederal.

King Edward II's tomb, Gloucester Cathederal.   *The Bishop Hooper Monument, Gloucester.*

Chapel has a mysterious, possibly pre-Christian, symbol of three fish in a triangle; and a knight can be seen in combat with a serpent and a winged dragon at the east end of the choir. There are numerous other interesting features, but probably the most poignant and haunting is the effigy of King Edward II, which surmounts his splendid tomb in the cathedral. Edward was murdered in a particularly awful way (see entry for Berkeley) and the effigy's face is said to have been copied from a death mask, indelibly imprinted with his final moments of agony. Certainly the effigy does not convey the impression of a noble king at peace.

Several locations in the vicinity of the cathedral are shrouded in tales of mystery and superstition. The Bishop Hooper Monument at St Mary's Square stands on the site of Bishop John Hooper's martyrdom in 1555. In the reign of King Henry VIII his opinions had necessitated his living in exile on the Continent, but on the accession of the Protestant King Edward VI he was in 1551 consecrated as Bishop of Gloucester. Tasked with reforming the church, he went on to find evidence of corruption and ignorance of the Christian faith, but when the king died and was replaced by the staunchly Catholic Queen Mary he found himself accused of responsibility for much of the corruption he had discovered. He was imprisoned and charged with heresy, and condemned to be burned at the stake. On 9 February 1555 he was taken to St. Mary's Square and bound with iron hoops to a stake around which stacks of timber and straw were piled, and it was demanded that he reject the Protestant faith in favour of Catholicism. He refused, and in front of a reported crowd of 7,000 the fire was lit. The straw and wood were damp and green, and the fire went out three times, greatly prolonging Hooper's agonies, so that he

Detail of the Bishop Hooper Monument, Gloucester.　　　　*St Mary's Arch, Gloucester.*

begged for 'more fire!'. Indeed, he is said to have endured the flames for three quarters of an hour before finally succumbing. It is said that Bishop Hooper's execution was watched by Queen Mary from the upstairs chamber of St. Mary's Arch, and that her ghost is sometimes seen there still.

If superstition, rumour and legend are to be believed, the phantom of Queen Mary is just one of numerous entities that appear in the city, and while these accounts will not stand up to any scientific examination they do at least provide an interesting snapshot of Gloucester's past and present folklore. Probably the most thorough collection of these stories is to be found in *Haunted Gloucestershire* by Rupert Matthews, but for the purposes of this work a brief description is thought sufficient.

Monks and priests might well be regarded as 'the usual suspects' where any account of ghostly activity is concerned, and at least three of the city's spectral phantoms fall into that category. A ghostly monk is said to have been seen close to St Michael's Gate, which leads to the cathedral precincts, while a phantom priest has been reportedly seen many times at St Mary de Lode Church, Archdeacon Street, close to the Bishop Hooper monument. This unfortunate priest was drowned at sea, apparently, when returning from a visit to Rome in the fourteenth century. Blackfriars Priory, off Gloucester's Southgate Street, is a former medieval Dominican friary that was dissolved by King Henry VIII in 1539. Here, it is said, a hideously-scarred phantom monk has been seen kneeling in prayer at what was once the high altar of the priory church.

Unfortunate children, too, are staple features of many ghost stories, and Gloucester is not without several such waifs. Phantom children are said to haunt the Folk Museum in Westgate Street, which, in the Victorian era, was a pin factory that employed children among its workforce. An orphan boy is supposed to haunt Church House in Cathedral Close and at Westgate Galleria in Westgate Street the ground floor is reportedly haunted by a little girl in Victorian garb – thought be an inmate of the workhouse that once stood there. Gambier Parry Lodge on the city's Tewkesbury Road stands on the site of a former Victorian hospital run by nuns, one of whom is said to have hanged herself after the death of a child in her care. It was subsequently reported that a phantom nun, with a small child in her arms, was seen in that part of the building.

Probably some of the most popular locations for incidences of haunting and apparently inexplicable activity are inns and public houses, and readers may well have their own suspicions about the origin of some experiences. The following is a brief résumé of Gloucester's best known inn-dwelling ghosts, although it is likely there are many more reports yet to be published. At The Dick Whittington Inn in Westgate Street the apparition of a man wearing a flat tweed cap has been seen many times in the bar, while the cellar is haunted by the ghost of a maid, said to have died there in the seventeenth century. Also in Westgate Street, the spectral figure of a lady in a blue dress was frequently reported at The Fleece Hotel during the 1960s and 1970s. Another phantom lady, this time dressed in white, has been seen many times walking along the upstairs corridors of The New Inn at Northgate Street – dating from the fourteenth century, The New Inn is actually anything but 'new'. The King's Head in the city's Gloucester Road claims to have three ghosts: a cavalier, a monk and a porter. Minor poltergeist activity at The Old Crown Inn in Westgate Street has over the years been attributed to the ghostly activities of Roundhead soldiers killed there during the Civil War, while poltergeist activity at the former Greyfriars Inn, off Southgate Street, in 1988 was considered to have been prompted by renovation work to the building. Paradoxically, poltergeist activity that had been present for years in The Kingsholm Inn, at Kingsholm Road to the north of the city centre, came to an abrupt end following renovation work in the 1980s.

Other miscellaneous ghosts include a helpful 'ghost butler' at Bishop's House, near the cathedral, the apparition of Lady Catherine Hayward – who is occasionally seen at a window of Bearland House in Southgate Street, wistfully gazing across the garden – and the ghost of young actress Eliza Johnson who haunts the former Theatre Royal in Westgate Street, following her suicide in 1880 while appearing in a play there. There are spectacular ghosts, too. Roman soldiers are supposed to have been seen in Denmark Road, and it is said that at the docks on still evenings a spectral Spanish ghost ship is sometimes seen – the bodies of two murdered Spaniards hanging from the yardarm.

Although the majority of Gloucester's mysteries concern tales of apparitions and poltergeists, there are several accounts of UFO sightings, and there are even reports of big cats being seen on the outskirts of the city. Lynn Picknett, in her publication *The Mammoth Book of UFOs*, describes how in 1978 a woman living just outside the city awoke in the early hours of the morning and, on looking out of the window, saw '…an enormous red object like a huge tower with six yellow lights, one beneath the other…' The woman called the police and an officer attended and saw the object for himself, apparently suggesting it might be a distant television mast. The woman dismissed this idea and continued to watch the UFO, which remained in the sky for another hour or so before disappearing from sight. A subsequent press report failed to attract other witnesses, and greater detail of the sighting – such as size and distance – seems not to have been obtained.

One evening in November 1996 a witness reported seeing a 'huge boomerang-shaped object' just below the clouds over Gloucester. He stated that the object was silent, bigger than a plane and left no vapour trail behind it. When the unusual shape of aircraft such as the Stealth bomber is considered, however, the suspicion must be that the object was a conventional – if unusual – aircraft.

At Hucclecote, on the south-eastern side of Gloucester, a very large UFO was seen by three independent witnesses in late 1999. A man taking his dog for a walk one evening noticed in the night sky a large white light, which had many different coloured lights moving in a shimmering effect within it. Additionally, what had at first appeared to be a star formation behind the white light was actually moving with the light, suggesting that all the lights were a part of a single UFO. The 'object' was estimated to be about a mile above the witness and was the size of an open newspaper held out at arm's length. A second man was seen watching the spectacle – he commented on its huge size and that it made no sound – and the original witness summoned his brother to see it. The three watched the UFO from a nearby motorway bridge, and it was then seen to move away and over a hill several miles distant. It seems that others, too, saw the object, as several reports were made to the local radio station the next day.

A man watching a police helicopter hovering above the city's Painswick Road roundabout one evening in 2001 was startled to see 'a large green ball' suddenly fly low across the sky and directly beneath the helicopter. Apparently the ball moved faster than a helicopter, but not quickly enough to be a shooting star. It does seem likely, however, that this object was actually a meteorite.

If claims of UFOs hovering in the skies above Gloucester make interesting reading it is likely that accounts of panther-like cats seen prowling in the vicinity of the city will be no less fascinating. According to reports, alien big cats were particularly active – or indiscreet – during the mid-1990s. In 1994, two witnesses were putting out rubbish in their garden near the Sharpness bypass when something snarled at them from the undergrowth; looking up at the motorway embankment at the rear of their house, they saw what looked like 'a huge cat loping off at great speed'. In the summer of the following year a woman heard the clamouring of birds in her back garden in the Barnwood suburb of Gloucester, and looking out of her window to investigate saw a 'large black cat' at the foot of her garden. The animal, which she stated was much bigger than an ordinary cat, then vaulted over a 5ft-fence bordering her neighbour's garden, before leaping over a 6ft-fence and disappearing into trees. The woman, who had been raised in the Forest of Dean and was familiar with wildlife, described the animal as 'like a young puma' with an 'exceedingly long and thick' tail. A resident of a nearby street also reported a similar sighting.

A country lane near Quedgeley, on the southern outskirts of the city, was the scene of the next encounter with a panther-like beast. A woman driving there in 1995 almost collided with an animal that ran out in front of her car. At first she thought it was a Doberman dog, but stated that it was 'bigger than that, more like a panther, black and sleek'. Finally, in the summer of that year, a man was night-fishing at a pond in the Matson area of the city when an animal emerged from some bushes about 30ft away. Assuming the beast to be canine, he soon realised that 'this was no dog', and shining a torch at it, judged it to be 'definitely from the cat family'. The animal, which was estimated at 2ft high and 4ft long, seemed not to be startled by the torch-light and 'just loped off' – possibly realising that a man fishing in a pond at night was unlikely to pose much of a threat.

GREAT BARRINGTON

There is little apparently mysterious about this charming village in the valley of the River Windrush, and although it is well within the territory of Oxfordshire's 'Beast of Burford' there are no known sightings of panther-like animals within the parish.

It has an idyllic hostelry, The Fox Inn, where en-suite accommodation is available, and it seems that the premises are haunted by the ghost of what might be a former maid. One room seems the focal point for the paranormal activity, and on one occasion in the 1990s a woman staying there awoke in the night to find the room bathed in a strange yellow 'glow'. Furthermore, the layout of the room had completely changed. Suddenly the apparitional figure of a woman wearing an old-fashioned maid's bonnet entered the room, bearing two cups of tea! The ghostly 'maid' left the cups of tea, then turned and left the room, without making any sound or acknowledgment of the room's occupant. On other occasions there has been minor poltergeist activity in the room, although the provision of phantom room service seems to have been a one-off occurrence.

GREAT RISSINGTON

There is a superstition in this village that a ghostly black dog is sometimes seen walking at midnight from the Barrington Road to the churchyard, where it descends into its master's grave. Apparently the dog has a heavy chain hanging from its neck, which has been heard chinking in the night. This tale was passed to the author in the 1980s, and even then the dog seemed not to have been actually seen within living memory. The story survives, however, as an example of local folklore.

Considerable alteration and renovation took place at Great Rissington's Manor House in the late 1980s, during which time contractors working in the building heard on several occasions the sounds of footsteps and voices coming from unoccupied rooms, leading to a belief that ghosts were responsible. The workmen enquired with the former occupants of the house, who said they did not believe the house to be haunted, but described curious incidents that happened occasionally. The family's small child would sometimes go missing in the house for longer than was desirable and, on reappearing, would be asked where she had been. She would always point to an area on the upper floor, apparently, adding that she had been with 'Sherman'. Curiously, this was the same area where the workmen had heard inexplicable voices and footsteps, although the identity of the mysterious 'Sherman' remains unknown.

GUITING POWER

The Church of St Michael has a 'green man' foliate head carving on a corbel in the chancel arch, which is of itself somewhat mysterious in that no one can be quite certain

what it symbolises – although a pagan representation of fertility and the regeneration of the human spirit is the usual explanation offered. The Guiting 'green man' is perhaps one of the less attractive examples in the County – its rather sinister-looking face is dominated by a large gaping mouth.

An occupant of Rock Cottage, in the Picadilly area of the village, witnessed the apparition of a Cavalier in the property during the early 1980s. Visible for around ten seconds, the figure was a grey monochrome in colour, although

'Green Man' at Guiting Power Church.

its boots were a dull red, with one toe noticeably scuffed. Although the 'Cavalier' figure wore a cloak and hat, he was rather unimposing, appearing tired and uneasy. Quite why a Cavalier would be in a small cottage in Guiting Power is a mystery.

HAILES

Following King Henry VIII's Dissolution of the Monasteries in 1539, all that now remains of the Cistercian monks' Hailes Abbey on the western edge of the Cotswolds are a series of low walls and parts of the cloisters. Despite this very visible evidence of wanton destruction, however, the place has an atmosphere of serenity and tranquillity, with perhaps a hint of wistful solitude.

The abbey was founded in 1246 by King Henry III's brother, Richard, Earl of Cornwall. When caught in a storm at sea, Richard had vowed to found a religious house if God saw fit to spare him. God and the sea proved merciful and, as promised, the place of worship was founded – Richard himself attending the consecration of the new abbey in 1251. The monks who lived there would probably have merely eked out a living from their sheep and endowments paid by neighbouring parishes had Richard's son, Edmund, not come to their assistance. He gave them a phial that was claimed to hold some of Christ's blood – indeed, the Pope himself had authenticated this.

Hailes Abbey rapidly became famous as one of the most popular pilgrimage destinations in England, with people visiting in their thousands to see the sacred phial, which was kept in a shrine in an extension specially built for the purpose. At the Dissolution, however, the phial was removed to London, where it was examined and found to contain not blood, but a mixture of saffron and honey.

For many years – even centuries – there have been stories of ghostly monks seen wandering among the ruins, and claims have been made that ethereal sounds of chanting have been heard at the abbey in the night. No one seems to have heard or seen ghostly monks within living memory, however, although the evocative ruins would probably be the ideal setting for the shadow-like figures of ghostly monks.

Hailes Abbey ruins.

Hampnett

An interesting feature known as the 'Hangman's Stone' can be seen near the old A40 road between Northleach and Cheltenham within the parish of Hampnett. The site actually consists of two stones: one, used as a stile, has been set into a dry stone wall, while the second, larger stone, is a rough-surfaced, holed slab that lies on its side nearby. The stones mark the junction of the parishes of Hampnett, Yanworth and Stowell and might have been chosen as boundary markers, which tends to suggest they are of quite some antiquity.

According to folklore, the 'Hangman's Stone' acquired its name after a sheep stealer, when climbing over the stile, fell and became entangled with the sheep he was stealing, thereby hanging himself. This seems a highly unlikely scenario, however, and it is much more probable that the stone marked the site of a gibbet. The stones are situated in a lonely, isolated and windswept spot and it is not difficult to imagine the main stone (about 7ft in length) standing upright on a moonlit night, an executed highwayman hanging from it. No reports of such a spectacle have been received, however, with ghostly activity being confined to the occasional appearance of a spectral horse and trap, said to have been seen years ago on the road nearby.

Hardwicke

Although an individual village in its own right, Hardwicke has virtually been absorbed into the outskirts of Gloucester city. There seems little in the way of paranormal or mysterious activity there, although a resident has reported seeing a substantial UFO in the sky above the village in the mid-1970s.

At the time of the sighting, the witness was a mere eight years of age. Looking out through a window from inside a house at Hardwicke one evening he saw 'a huge craft' travelling in the air above a field behind the house. He called his brother and sister and all three were able to observe the UFO, which by this time was almost directly overhead. The object was estimated to be a 100ft above the observers and was 'the size of a football pitch', with the appearance of a flying hovercraft. As the UFO passed over the roof of the house, the three ran through to the other side of the building to get a better view – by which time the thing had completely vanished.

How much credibility should this account be afforded? Logic and one's day-to-day experiences make it seem incredible, but to dismiss it as fantasy might be considered rather too judgemental. It is not unlikely, however, that stories such as this will become the folklore of tomorrow.

Hyde

Inns and pubs are undoubtedly favourite locations for reports of mysterious and paranormal activity, although in many cases the accounts suggest little more than the frequent tipping over of beer glasses by some 'unseen force'. Perhaps unsurprisingly, many regard such pub-based stories with scepticism. It makes a change, then, for an inn to have a history that supports accounts of rather more than the usual ghostly shadows and accident-prone beer glasses.

One such pub is The Ragged Cot Inn at Hyde, near Minchinhampton. In 1760, when trade at the inn was at a low ebb, the landlord, one Bill Clavers, turned to crime to acquire additional funds. He took to robbing the night coach to London, and one night, in a state of violent drunkenness, he picked up his pistols and made to leave the home and await the coach. At the top of the stairs his wife tried to stop him – one account states that she was heavily pregnant, another that she was holding their baby in her arms. Clavers would have none of it and, pushing her violently, caused her to fall down the stairs. He rode off and carried out the robbery but, on returning with the constables hot on his trail, found his wife and child dead at the foot of the stairs. Realising his crimes included murder as well as robbery, he hid the bodies in a trunk, and opened fire when the constables arrived. Hearing a cry of terror come from within, however, they forced an entry and arrested Clavers. While trying to hide the bodies, it seems, he had seen the ghosts of his wife and child cross the room and ascend the stairs. As one of the constables discovered the bodies, a second officer saw a woman holding a baby, apparently watching the scene from across the room. Clavers was subsequently hanged at Gloucester.

The Ragged Cot, Hyde.

It is said that the ghosts of the mother and child still haunt the inn and former licensees have reported seeing the apparition of a woman in period clothes near the cellar. Sinister noises were heard coming from the cellar, too, and the landlord's dog refused to go near the cellar entrance. The ghosts have not been seen for some years, however, although in 2006 the landlady stated that inexplicable events were common – door handles would turn of their own accord, rapping and banging sounds were sometimes heard, and her pet dogs would react strongly to 'something', although there was no obvious stimulus.

KEMPSFORD

All of the mysterious happenings around the village of Kempsford, situated in the south-eastern corner of Gloucestershire, are centred on legends and ancient ghost stories that are loosely based on what are thought to be actual events. Each of these tales is well described in the very useful book *Haunted Gloucestershire* by Rupert Matthews.

The oldest ghost said to haunt Kempsford goes back to the times of the Viking invasions of the ninth century. During this turbulent period, one Oswyn, an English nobleman from

Churchyard tombs, Kempsford.

Kempsford, was approached by a Viking named Hengstan, who lived in nearby Wiltshire. According to the story Hengstan had fallen in love with Oswyn's niece, Ina, and sought permission to marry her. Far from granting permission, however, Oswyn horsewhipped Hengstan within an inch of his life, tied him to a maddened horse, and sent him back to Wiltshire. But if he thought that was the end of the matter, he was much mistaken. The Viking returned with a small army, slaughtered Oswyn – who could blame him? – and his servants, put his property to the torch, then rode off into the sunset with young Ina – with whom he lived happily ever after in Wiltshire. Tradition has it that Hengstan's ghost – complete with sword and horned helmet – is sometimes seen in the early morning walking along the banks of the River Ray at Kempsford.

Dating from the fourteenth century, the next two ghosts in the village are quite modern when compared with Hengstan. The first of these concerns a ghostly monk who is sometimes seen in the churchyard, but is more often seen at the site of the now vanished Kempsford Castle in the area between the church and the River Ray. According to legend, the fourteenth-century owner of the castle went off to fight in France, leaving his wife to look after the estate. The wife's brother, meanwhile, had fallen out with the king and turned up at the castle seeking refuge. She spirited him away in a secret chamber, but the servants' tongues wagged, and it is not difficult to imagine the sort of salacious gossip that probably circulated. This reached the ears of the castle's owner – who promptly returned and slaughtered both brother and sister. When he realised his terrible mistake he took on the lifestyle of a monk, seeking forgiveness for his sins. It is his sad ghost that supposedly wanders the area still.

Finally there is the ghost of Lady Maud, who, like Hengstan, wanders the banks of the river. Lady Maud and her husband, Henry Plantagenet, Duke of Lancaster, took possession of Kempsford in 1355, residing in their home beside the River Ray with their son and two daughters. Tragedy struck when the boy was drowned, however, and the duke was so heart-broken that he left the village, vowing never to return. Lady Maud remained in Kempsford, often wandering the banks of the river in sad contemplation, until she died soon after. It is said that her apparition, in a long dress, is still seen from time to time. Indeed, her ghost was reportedly seen as recently as 2001.

KINGSWOOD

According to local folklore, a woman lived at the sixteenth-century gatehouse of Kingswood Abbey in the 1830s and believed there to be a goblin under the floor. This 'goblin' was known to perform acrobatics with flagstones in the building, and was believed responsible for tipping chairs over. It seems likely that the strange activities were actually the result of a poltergeist. The abbey itself was demolished many years ago, but the gatehouse remains standing and is open to the public.

Kingswood House is now only a few ruins, with a new house built within them, but when it was an occupied building there were several apparitions connected with it. A phantom stagecoach has apparently been seen driving up to the house and circling the building, and a ghostly lady in grey was seen to enter the house after approaching from the village. The place even had a canine ghost, with the apparition of a black dog being seen to leave the main entrance to the building and walk to a field

Abbey Gatehouse, Kingswood.

opposite. These stories are merely local folklore traditions, however, and as the house has been demolished for years, it seems unlikely that the apparitions will appear again.

LECHLADE

This small town on the road between Burford and Cirencester has a couple of minor mysteries centred on Burford Street. Burford House, a former coaching inn, is supposed to have a secret tunnel that leads to the parish church, and high up on the external wall of the nearby Swan Inn is the distinct carving of a phallus! This is not a case of modern graffiti and its origin is unknown, but nevertheless intriguing.

The Royal Oak pub in Oak Street is believed by some to be haunted by the ghost of a former landlord. One customer reported seeing the apparition of the man walking across the bar, while another is said to have seen the landlord's face in one of the central supporting pillars of the bar. Whether copious consumption of the pub's ales assisted with this paranormal experience is not known.

LEONARD STANLEY

An Augustinian monastery was founded at Leonard Stanley in 1121, although this was closed down in the Reformation, and the old monastic church, which had been completed in 1129, was rededicated in favour of St Swithun.

Thought to be connected with the former monastery is a hooded spectre that is seen from time to time in the churchyard. It has been speculated that this phantom monk returns in spectral form to demonstrate his displeasure at the rededication of the church. Although there are no reports of a recent sighting of the monk, the haunting is locally well known, and it is possible that the apparition may be seen again when circumstances are favourable.

LITTLE WASHBOURNE

The Hobnails Inn at Little Washbourne apparently has a resident poltergeist, known to staff and regular customers as 'Harry'. This mischievous ghost performs the usual tricks, such as throwing ashtrays across the bar, turning on lights and opening doors. Roy Palmer, in his book *Folklore of Gloucestershire*, describes the troublesome activity that occurred during rewiring of the pub in 1989. Electricians' materials and tools left overnight in an attic were found strewn about the place the following morning.

This kind of thing has, apparently, become an accepted feature of the pub. Other pubs in Gloucestershire – such as The Fox at Broadwell and The Black Bear Inn at Moreton-in-Marsh – have similar poltergeists that are sporadically active.

LITTLEDEAN

The village of Littledean has been occupied since ancient times, with the remains of a Roman temple visible in the grounds of Littledean Hall, and there are a number of old buildings that date back as far as the seventeenth century. Having been continuously occupied since 1080, Littledean Hall is reputed to be the oldest inhabited house in England, and is full of interest. The present house – which is in private ownership and not open to the public – was built in the seventeenth century, with neo-Jacobean remodelling occurring in the mid-nineteenth century – although the building actually stands on Roman foundations.

Given the long occupancy of the house, it is not surprising that several ghosts are said to haunt the place. In 1644, when Royalist soldiers garrisoned the house, Roundhead troops stormed the building and, after a savage swordfight, killed two of the officers in the dining room. The ghosts of the two Royalist officers have occasionally been seen there since, apparently, and tradition has it that to this day their bloodstains remain on the floor, apparently re-appearing even when the floorboards have been replaced. The occupant of the house during this period was one Richard Brayne, who, during the military occupancy in the Civil War, disguised himself as Littledean Hall's gardener to avoid arrest. His ghost is supposed to have been seen – most recently in the 1980s – in the drive, sweeping away leaves.

In 1744 Charles Pyrke, whose family then lived at the Hall, was murdered at the age of twenty-three by a black servant who discovered that Pyrke had fathered the servant's sister's child – the baby had been found dead behind panelling in either the Blue or Rose Room (accounts differ). The servant was convicted of murder and hanged, and it is claimed that his ghost, carrying a lighted candle, has been seen many times outside the drawing room and outside what was his bedroom.

There are other ghosts, too. A ghostly monk is said to walk from the library to the dining room, where it is claimed there was a priest's hole that led to a tunnel from the cellar to the Grange of Flaxley Abbey.

Not far from Littledean Hall, the lane that runs to Newnham was supposed to be haunted by the apparitions of two women dressed in grey or white. These rather vague and blurred images were reported by a number of witnesses. In the twentieth century, the sightings ended, if the reports are to be believed, after workmen widening the lane discovered two buried female skeletons. It was determined, it seems, that the bodies were over a century old, and the bones were given 'a decent reburial'. Accounts of these ghostly manifestations differ, however. Rupert Matthews, in *Haunted Gloucestershire*, states that the skeletons were discovered in 1932 and that 'the ghosts are as active as ever'. Anthony Poulton-Smith, in *Paranormal Cotswolds*, however, says the bones were found in the 1970s and that sightings of the two women have stopped.

Probably the most noticeable building in the village is Littledean Jail. Built in 1791, it was used as a 'House of Correction' until 1954, although it had been used as a Police Station, Remand Prison and Petty Sessional Court from 1874. A rather forbidding looking building of red sandstone that looks as though it ought to be haunted by the tortured souls of long-dead prisoners, there is in fact a report of just one resident ghost. Apparently there is a little ghost-boy who pushes through crowds of visitors and pulls at ladies' skirts.

Littledean House Hotel is thought to date from the early seventeenth century, originally having been a row of cottages that has been added to over the years. Sue Law, in *Ghosts of the Forest of Dean*, describes how a landing in the oldest part of the house is known as 'Fred's Landing'. The atmosphere is always very cold there, apparently, and people have complained of paranormal sensations – including being shoved by some unseen force, forced to press against a wall to allow 'something' to pass, and the feeling of being crowded-in. In the latter years of the twentieth century the apparition of a man wearing a long black cape and a large velvet cap was seen.

Finally, a building known as the Red House is of interest. Parts of the building are possibly Norman and the house has had a varied and sometimes turbulent history. Oak panelling in the dining room bears bullet holes from the civil war, and in the nineteenth century the house became the village workhouse. On a number of occasions each year during the last decade of the twentieth century, residents in the dining room saw a tall, thin man, wearing a wide-brimmed black hat, pass through the gate outside, without opening it, and fade away. The apparition carried out the exact procedure on numerous occasions, vanishing before anyone could go outside to greet 'him'. The house was at one time used for Quaker meetings, and it is thought that perhaps the apparition is connected with that period.

LONGBOROUGH

The discovery of two human skeletons, unearthed during the creation of a driveway to the front of The New Rectory, caused a brief wave of excitement among local police officers in 1983 – although enthusiasm soon dissipated when the bones were judged to be greatly in excess of a hundred years old. One of the skeletons was much smaller than the other, which led some to speculate that the remains were those of a mother and child.

Who these people were remains a minor mystery. The skeletons were not found near any graveyard or burial site, and it was suggested that they were possibly plague victims, buried hastily and unceremoniously to avoid further contamination. There again, they may have been the victims of a highwayman, or, indeed, some other type of foul play. All that is certain is that their fate and identities will remain a mystery.

There are no known sightings of UFOs or big cats in the village, but Longborough does have several ghost stories. During the late 1970s and early 1980s the apparition of an old man wearing a raincoat was seen on a number of occasions by witnesses (including a dog!) inside Mullion Cottage in the village High Street. The figure was each time seen to walk past a window at the back of the cottage, although it appeared to be at a higher level than the existing outside path. Every member of the family saw the figure, and the dog reacted to its presence by barking and moving towards the window. The higher level that the apparition seemed to follow was subsequently explained when it was found that the original path at the back of the cottage had been replaced by a path that was several feet lower. The ghost has not been seen for years, however, and it seems that – for whatever reason – it was simply following a course that had been regularly followed through life. Perhaps factors, such as atmospheric conditions, played a part.

Longborough has two pubs – both named The Coach and Horses – although one of them is situated in a part of the village called Ganborough. This part of the village is certainly not of a size that would merit it being called a separate hamlet. Both pubs have seen a degree of paranormal activity, although in each case it seemed centred more on the individuals than on the buildings. The landlady of the pub in the centre of the village experienced several minimally odd occurrences

Mullion Cottage, Longsborough.

in the 1980s. A row of glasses hanging above the bar started to swing slowly from side to side late one night after all of the customers had left, although there was no draught that could have caused this to happen. On several occasions a radio in the bar inexplicably switched itself on, then late one night when the landlady was upstairs she clearly heard a voice call her name from downstairs in the bar area. Investigation failed to locate any person, however, and the matter remained a puzzle.

A woman asleep in bed one night at the pub in the Ganborough part of the village apparently experienced unwelcome attention in the mid-1980s. She was suddenly awoken by the alarming sensation of 'someone' lifting the mattress and tucking the bedclothes in. There was no one in the room, nor any apparent cause, and terrified, the woman began to recite the Lord's Prayer. At this, the sensation stopped instantly and the heavy door of a nearby wardrobe suddenly opened violently. This sounds very much like the ingredients of a nightmare, but the woman is adamant the incident actually happened, and subsequent conversation with a previous occupant of the inn revealed that the apparition of an old woman had been seen in the room some years earlier.

By the early years of the twenty-first century a different licensee was running the pub and no unusual experiences have been reported. As recently as 2009, however, a curious incident occurred in the public bar. A customer was seated at a table when he saw a friendly-looking King Charles spaniel run across the floor of the room and under the table near his feet. He reached under the table to pat the dog but could not feel it, so stood up and looked carefully to see where the animal might be hiding. It quickly became clear that no dog was there, or anywhere else in the bar, and the man grew quite unnerved as he realised that he must have seen an apparition or 'ghost dog'.

LONGNEY

The only mysterious accounts that have come to light about this village near the River Severn concern sightings of a large black beast reported in 1993. A man was walking home to the village one night along the banks of the river when he was suddenly confronted by a 'huge black creature with blazing green eyes'. The beast growled at him, then ran off across a field, apparently covering about 5 acres in 10 seconds! Initially only about 6ft away, the terrified witness described it as around 3ft long and 2ft high, and 'definitely a big cat with very large teeth'.

The credibility of this report is increased by a further report, this time from a Longney couple who had seen the animal pounce in front of their car a week earlier. They described it as 'a big black animal with a long tail' and 'massive green eyes'. During the same period a goose disappeared and a duck was found dead with its head bitten off at The Ship Inn at Longney, this incident causing further speculation about a big cat in the area.

LOWER SWELL

This must have been an important place in ancient times. Barrows that form the remains of a Bronze Age cemetery are concentrated on an area called Cow Common, beside the minor road to Guiting Power. In all there are ten round barrows as well as one long barrow from the earlier Neolithic period. This place was clearly very significant to the people of that time and although cremations and skeletal remains were revealed during the somewhat rudimentary nineteenth-century examination of the graves, there is no evidence to suggest any of those buried was of great importance. Also of interest is a megalith known as the Hoar Stone, this time in a meadow beside the road to Upper Slaughter. Measuring about 6ft in length by 3ft in height, the stone stands isolated in the field, with no obvious sign that it ever formed part of a burial chamber.

A stone known as The Whittlestone is also of interest, not only for its historical significance, but for the local folklore connected with it. This scarred and pitted stone measures about 5ft by 4½ft and lies on the roadside verge next to the village hall. It is all that remains of a Neolithic long barrow that once stood on a hill near the church, the stone having many years ago been pulled from the ground and placed in the vicarage paddock, before it was decided to place it at its present location. As with so many ancient stones, the Whittlestone is credited in a local tradition with the ability to move. When it hears Stow-on-the-Wold church clock strike twelve midnight, it is said, the stone goes to the nearby Lady's Well to drink. The well stands beside the driveway to a fine house, named Abbotswood, and is apparently the destination of another supernatural entity. A ghostly figure known as The Grey Lady is said to walk from the village church to Lady's Well at midnight. A local man has reported how, as a youngster in the 1960s, he saw the hazy figure of The Grey Lady near the well. He always understood the figure to be that of a nun who collects water from the well.

More recently, there have been reports of how an elderly lady living at a house in Fox Drive saw the apparitions of several figures in the house during the 1980s. Each appearance was preceded by a sensation of intense cold, the figures seeming completely lifelike until they suddenly vanished. Finally, a story of inexplicable activity came to the author from a particularly reliable source some time ago. The person concerned, a respected local historian, described how as a boy in the late 1940s he attended a school at Nether Swell Manor, near the village. An old wooden harmonium stood in the main hall, being used to supply the music for Sunday services. It had been given to the school by a local benefactor who had been fond of playing it, and had apparently been actually playing it when he suddenly died. Stories of the instrument being played when no one was at the keyboard were common, and on one occasion he was woken at night by the sound of the harmonium playing in the hall below. It was quickly ascertained that no one was in the hall at the time, nor was the tune recognized by any of the boys. There was at least one other odd incident involving the organ, but having outlived its useful life, it was no longer being used by the mid-1960s.

The Whittlestone, Lower Swell.

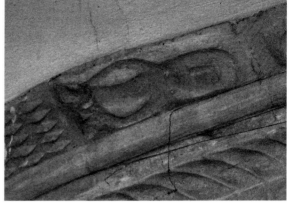

Lady's Well, Lower Swell.   *Sheela-na-Gig at Lower Swell Church.*

It was reported in the mid-1990s that The Golden Ball Inn was haunted by a 'shouting' ghost. Years earlier, apparently, the ghostly figure of an old man smoking a pipe was seen in a rocking chair in an upstairs room at the inn. It seems, however, that the ghost is more often heard than seen, and on numerous occasions unintelligible shouting has been heard coming from various parts of the building. This has always been attributed to the activities of the ghost, the 'shouting ghost' having become such a regular feature that he has been given the nickname of 'Fred'. Although one woman working at the inn became so alarmed by the shouting that she quit her employment there, 'Fred' seems to have become accepted by most of the pub regulars as a curious and amusing feature.

Finally, a strange and somewhat mysterious feature can be seen at the Church of St Mary. Of Norman date, a crudely carved Sheela-na-Gig exhibitionist figure is displayed on one of the archways. These nude figures are often described as 'pagan fertility symbols', although their real purpose is something of a mystery. (*See* also entry for Ampney St Peter.)

LYDBROOK

This large and tranquil village next to the Wye Valley was for hundreds of years a busy industrial centre, but is nowadays much used as a base by tourists visiting both the Forest of Dean and Wye Valley areas.

There seems little that is mysterious about the place, and there are just two folklore accounts. Roy Palmer, in his book *Folklore of Gloucestershire*, mentions that a house named Bet Kebir in the village is known as 'Ghost House' because a figure in riding attire is seen walking down the stairs, and Sue Law, in *Ghosts of the Forest of Dean*, describes how the ghost of a girl whose unrequited love led her to commit suicide has been seen standing outside a cottage beside the old railway line.

LYDNEY

A small town on the banks of the River Severn, Lydney and its harbour on the Lydney Canal was once important as a transhipment point for timber, coal and iron brought from the Forest of Dean. Of considerable interest at the town's Lydney Park is a fourth-century Roman Temple to Nodens, a Celtic divinity. It is thought to have been a healing shrine and a mosaic there bore an inscription that referred to 'Victorinus the Interpreter', probably an interpreter of dreams. Author Danny Sullivan, in his book *Ley Lines*, describes how visitors to the temple would sleep and dream there, then, 'a therapeute would listen to them recounting their previous night's dreams and make predictions based upon them'.

After the Romans left England, however, the temple fell into disrepair and ruin, and the local people began to believe that it was home to dwarfs and hobgoblins. J.R.R. Tolkien, writer of *Lord of the Rings*, was one of the team that excavated the site in the 1920s, and it is believed that he may have used his knowledge of such folk tales in his stories of Middle Earth.

There are two ghost stories centred on Lydney. The first of these concerns an ancient tradition that a local murderer, William Morgan, haunts Naas Lane. One evening in the summer of 1771, Morgan, having gambled away all his money, decided to acquire some more by committing robbery. Two local women – a Miss Jones of Naas House, and her friend, Miss Gough – walked past him, and he determined to rob them of whatever money they had, so began to follow them. At one point he passed them, and Miss Jones, recognising him, wished him goodnight. It seems to have been the realisation that his intended victims knew him that prompted him to carry out not just robbery, but murder. Morgan then came up behind the women and struck Miss Jones two heavy blows with a stick, killing her, then chased after Miss Gough and struck her in the same way, leaving her lying seriously injured in a ditch.

Morgan rifled through his victims' pockets, stealing some cash and a small pocket knife. In doing this, he got blood on his breeches. Soon there was a commotion in the area, with local men being ordered to search for the murderer. When Morgan answered the call, the blood was seen on his breeches and he confessed to the crime. Tried and convicted, he was no doubt hanged for his deeds. His ghost has been seen on many occasions near Naas House, although there are no reports of any recent sightings.

In the middle of the twentieth century a local woman is supposed to have seen the figures of three monks, in long black cloaks with cowls over their heads, walking in what is now Driffield Road. The woman was with her boyfriend at the time, and on seeing the strange sight they hurried past the silent monks. Then, looking back, the couple discovered that the monks had completely vanished.

MAUGERSBURY

A local tradition has it that this very small hamlet is connected to the nearby town of Stow-on-the-Wold by a secret tunnel that leads underground from Maugersbury Manor to the King's Arms Hotel in Stow's market square. Both buildings are very old – the oldest parts of Maugersbury Manor are considered to date to the later years of the sixteenth century, and the house probably stands on the site of an earlier house belonging to Evesham Abbey, recorded in 1402; and The King's Arms Hotel was an inn by 1647.

Maugersbury Manor was used as a regional headquarters by American troops during the Second World War, and a local resident has claimed that servicemen discovered hidden vaults beyond the cellars and, when exploring them, found a tunnel that lead towards Stow-on-the-Wold. Apparently the servicemen followed the tunnel for some distance, but after a while found it blocked. The man relating this account remembers exploring around the manor as a boy soon after the war, and recalls seeing the vaults but declined to search for the tunnel.

It seems unlikely – but not impossible – that such a tunnel actually exists. The ground beneath Stow-on-the-Wold, however, is widely believed to be a labyrinth of tunnels, and photographic evidence of at least one such passageway or vault certainly exists.

may HILL

The tree-topped mass of May Hill is among Gloucestershire's most recognisable landmarks, and is visible for miles around as one approaches from the north, south or east. Certainly the little village of the same name halfway up its slope is considerably lesser known than the hill itself.

Several ghosts are supposed to have been seen in the vicinity of the village, including a white-bearded old man who walks near the chapel, and a figure that wanders in Folly Lane, carrying a red lantern. Glasshouse Hill, between May Hill and the village of Huntley, is said to have a spectral figure that follows anyone walking up the hill by the light of the moon.

Tales of pagan activity at May Hill are not uncommon, and in the early years of the twentieth century there were claims of witchcraft being practised there. As with so many of the county's hills and landmarks, there have long been tales of buried treasure and secret tunnels at the hill. It has been recorded that in the nineteenth century there certainly was a cavern in a field forming part of Great Cugley Farm, to the north-east of the hill, although there is no trace of it today. It is said that a second underground chamber existed some 500 metres to the south-east of the summit of the hill, and in 1884 an elderly Newent woman recalled playing in the cave when she was a child. Again, there is no longer any trace of the chamber.

It was believed that a subterranean passage linked these two chambers and that buried treasure was concealed somewhere along the tunnel. Although the existence of the chambers seems possible, there is little evidence of a tunnel joining the two, and still less of any hidden treasure. Even today, the story persists in the form of local folklore.

MICKLETON

For hundreds of years the best known ghost story associated with the village has been that of the strangely-named 'Mickleton Hooter'. The ghost is far more often heard than seen and gives out a moaning, screeching sound – likened by some to the bark of a dog or the sound made by a vixen. Some claim to have seen it, however, describing it as a tall, white figure. At least one description claimed it to resemble a calf with a man's head. There are no recent reports of the Hooter being heard or seen, and it seems that the story has now become a local folklore tradition.

So, where might one experience the sound of the Mickleton Hooter? The village of Hidcote Bartrim – famed for its beautiful Manor Garden – stands above Mickleton, at the edge of an escarpment that plunges down to the village below. This wooded valley, from where there are splendid views of the Evesham Vale beyond, is known as Weeping Hollow, and this is where the Hooter has most commonly been heard. The most plausible explanation for the strange noise points out that the steep sides of the valley may create a kind of funnel, which might distort or amplify the whistling sounds made by the wind.

Inevitably, stories to account for the ghost have circulated throughout the years. There is a legend that, centuries ago, villages in nearby Warwickshire were terrorised by a huge, savage cow – 'The Dun Cow' – that belonged to a giant. This monstrous beast was slain by

Weeping Willow, Mickleton.

the folk hero Guy of Warwick. Some have claimed that it is this cow – or its ghost – that haunts Weeping Hollow.

There is a story, too, that says the wailing ghost of Sir Edward Greville's son is sometimes heard there. In the sixteenth century Greville killed his son at Weeping Hollow, having mistaken him for a robber. The story of the accidental death is varied in another account, which states that Sir Edward shot an arrow high up into the air from a strong bow – the arrow plummeting down onto the head of his brother (not his son) and killing him.

MINCHINHAMPTON

The area around Minchinhampton is rich in ancient history, with much evidence still visible of our ancient ancestors. To the south-east of the village, close to the road from Avening, is the Long Stone – probably the best known megalith in the county. This ancient stone, which stands about 8ft high, is of oolite limestone and has two holes running through it. Years ago, babies would be passed through the larger of the holes in the belief that the procedure was a cure for smallpox and rickets. Other traditional folklore beliefs are that the stone runs around the field when it hears the church clock strike twelve, and that it goes down to the spring at Minchinhampton. Dowsers carrying out experiments near the stone have found that it somehow interferes with the local magnetic field, causing fluctuations in energy readings.

The stretch of road that runs past the Long Stone and a couple of nearby farms just outside the village are known as Woefuldane Bottom. This name is said to commemorate an ancient battle that took place near the Long Stone between the Saxons and the Danes, where the casualties were so great that blood ran freely in the fields. This account certainly makes for an evocative scene, but the true origin of the name is thought to be rather more prosaic: 'woeful' has been suggested as a corruption of the name Wulfflaed, while 'dene' means 'valley way'.

Quite apart from its reputation as the scene of a bloody battle, however, Woefuldane Bottom is said to be the haunt of a headless black dog, described by a couple of local residents in the 1970s. Roy Palmer, in his book *Folklore of Gloucestershire*, states that, years ago, carters passing along the location would blindfold their horses for fear that a phantom black dog would startle them. Ghostly figures have been seen, apparently, as well as phantom-hounds, and in the 1950s walkers became perturbed by the sight of a 'tall figure' following some distance behind them. In his book *Haunted Gloucestershire*, Rupert Matthews mentions a lady in a long dress who stands beside the road from Minchinhampton to Avening, staring anxiously at passing vehicles.

Some historians believe that a stone circle known as The Devil's Churchyard once existed on Cherrington Common, to the south-east of Minchinhampton (see entry for Cherington – just one 'r' in this spelling). Local clergy had these stones removed, it is said, and taken to Lammas House at Minchinhampton, and what is left of these stones may still be seen there today.

A well known landmark, where five roads meet on lonely and windswept Minchinhampton Common, is Tom Long's Post. It is supposed to be the burial place of a local suicide victim of that name, although an alternative version of the legend states that Tom Long was a notorious highwayman who was caught and hanged at a gibbet that is reputed to have stood at the site. Some accounts embellish the yarn by adding that – whether suicide or highwayman – Long was buried at the spot and his corpse pinned to the ground by a stake. Some claim that Tom Long's ghost haunts the area around the signpost, although as no witness has been identified this may well be fanciful invention or superstition.

Tom Long's Post, Minchinhampton Common.

Finally, there is a local tradition that the lane running from Minchinhampton to The Weighbridge Inn, a little to the south of the village, is haunted by the ghostly spectre of a man who was found there in the later years of the eighteenth century, having died in unexplained circumstances. The sudden appearance of this apparition is always portentous, signifying that within a year a member of the witness's family will die.

MORETON-IN-MARSH

Paranormal activity and folklore beliefs seem very much alive and well at Moreton-in-Marsh. Indeed, a veritable plethora of tales exists and, while the majority concern ghosts and incidences of haunting, sightings of UFOs and what may have been a panther have been claimed, too.

Some of the tales are based on very old local traditions that have been passed on through the generations. It is likely, for example, that parents years ago would warn their children about ghosts and haunted houses in order to ensure they came home before darkness fell. Many years ago it was locally 'well known' that a ghost would come out of a wall at the edge of the churchyard in Church Street and float across the road before disappearing into Lilac Cottage. There are no recent reports of any such ghost having been seen, however. In Oxford Street, not far away, stands the imposing Lemington House – another place that has for many years been supposedly haunted. A ghostly woman is said to have been seen peering from an upstairs window when the house was known to be unoccupied and in the later years of the twentieth century a strong scent of orange blossom would suddenly become apparent in a room on the first floor. Although far from unwelcome, the scent's arrival seemed quite inexplicable and rather mysterious.

Beyond Lemington House, Oxford Street becomes London Road and crosses a bridge over the railway line that runs from Oxford to Worcester. Several tales centred on this part of the town exist, although in every case it is many years since the experiences occurred. The claim that a headless cyclist was once seen passing over the bridge might raise a smile in some quarters, although it is thought unlikely to be considered among the most believable ghost stories in the district. Strange, unearthly noises are said to have been heard in the vicinity of the former turnpike house near the foot of the bridge, and unidentified noises apparently used to be heard sometimes coming from a former gasworks that once stood close to Oddfellows Terrace. Until the First World War years a golf course used to exist on land to the east of the railway station nearby, and a story exists of how, as a boy of twelve, a local resident saw a grey, ashen-faced phantom hovering through a hedge there. This ominous apparition appeared at a point where the boy would usually have expected to see his father tending the course and later, when his father was killed at war in France, the boy believed it to have been a premonition of his father's death.

Years later, a motorcyclist travelling along the London Road near what is today the Fire Service College claimed to have seen a ghostly white spectre following him along the road. Fortunately, the motorcycle appeared capable of greater speed than the spectre, for it was soon left behind. It may be that the spectre was in fact an unusual formation of fog or mist.

Inns and public houses often seem to be the favoured dwelling places of ghosts, and many observers may consider this to be more to do with the power of alcoholic beverages than with the paranormal. Yet a number of incidences of haunting of this kind are quite well documented, and some poltergeists, in particular, are so active that it seems overly cynical to regard every account as a product of invention or inebriation. Moreton's licensed premises certainly seem to have more than their fair share of ghostly residents and, while some tales are almost certainly folklore accounts based on superstition, others are quite convincing. The White Hart Royal Hotel is among the town's oldest buildings and King Charles I is believed to have spent the night there on 2 July 1644. It is no surprise, then, that a night porter once claimed to have seen a Cavalier, complete with plumed headwear, walk across a room and straight through a wall. There have been other reports of a ghostly male figure being seen in the bar area, and there are the usual claims of doors opening and closing of their own accord. One room, in particular, was the scene of unrest one night in 1988. A couple staying there were troubled by the sound of cupboards being opened in the room, and of footsteps going into the toilet. The cause of this activity was never identified.

Moreton's rather grand Manor House Hotel, which dates in part to 1545, has long been reputed haunted. For most of its existence it has been a private house, not becoming a hotel until just before the Second World War, and for well over a hundred years the property was leased by the Creswyke family, who can be traced to the Royal Family. In 1752, however, the house was sold at a low price because it was considered haunted by the ghost of Dame Creswyke, who is supposed to have come to a sticky end there. It was said that shadows seen through cracks in one of the doors re-played the way in which she met her untimely death. She was murdered at the house, so legend has it, either by strangulation or by drowning. The room where one account claims she was murdered was the scene of numerous strange occurrences in the 1980s. These included poltergeist activity and the sighting of an apparitional lady, seen sitting at the foot of the bed and combing her hair. Poltergeist activity has occurred elsewhere in the building, too, and in the late 1980s a couple walking along the High Street saw a lady in a long, flowing dress enter the hotel by walking straight through a wall.

Ghostly footsteps were often heard in the corridor outside a particular room in The Redesdale Arms Hotel through the 1970s and 1980s, and at The Bell Inn in the centre of Moreton several people have reported a ghost that 'hugged' them in one of the bedrooms there. This ghost has never actually been seen, but has for years been considered that of an amorous former landlord, known to have hade an eye for the ladies.

It is at The Black Bear Inn, however, that Moreton's busiest ghost resides. For at least thirty years a poltergeist nicknamed 'Fred' has made its appearance known to staff and customers, and there are numerous accounts of strange occurrences. Inanimate objects have suddenly been thrown through the air by some unseen force, pictures have fallen off walls, bottles have been knocked off shelves, electrical appliances have turned themselves off and on, and water has suddenly gushed from taps. Bunches of keys have gone missing, then, minutes later, suddenly reappeared. 'Fred' has been seen by a number of people – but only ever in the form of a shadowy, hazy image, fleetingly glimpsed – and eerie footsteps have been heard pacing in the kitchen. The strange activities seem to come and go in phases, and sometimes nothing unusual happens for a year or so, but at other times there can be a number of incidents over a short period. The poltergeist behaviour is rarely of major concern, although on one occasion in the 1990s, when a very heavy frying pan was hurled across the inn's kitchen, it was thought that the services of a priest may be needed. Fortunately, the overly-energetic activity subsided and 'Fred' has been relatively inactive for a few years. He did make his presence known again in the early years of the twenty-first century, however, when two people standing in the bar suddenly heard the inn's organ briefly burst into life. For many years The Black Bear Inn possessed an organ that stood in one corner and was played on Sunday evenings to an appreciative audience of young sweethearts and senior citizens. The organ was removed from the inn during the mid-1980s, so it was with considerable surprise that its distinctive tones were heard in the bar some twenty years later!

The only spirits to be found at the town's other inns and pubs are those in bottles on the shelves, although a former licensee of The Wellington Inn reported sensing an unnerving 'presence' at the inn during the early years of the twenty-first century. Sinister rapping sounds, too, heightened the feeling of disquiet. This seems to have been an isolated case, however, and no further reports have been received.

Two ladies occupied in cleaning the interior of Orchard Cottage in East Street were startled in the early 1970s when the sound of heavy footsteps was heard on the stairs, although no one else was in the building. Curiously, a swirling cloud of what looked and smelt like pipe tobacco was detected around the foot of the stairs. Unlike this pipe-smoking ghost, however, ghosts seen in a bedroom of The Old Parsonage in nearby Church Street on two occasions in 1964 were engaged in silent prayer. A woman sleeping in the house at that time first saw a priest, in brown habit, kneeling in prayer at a bed near her own, then, a few months later, she again saw a priest in the room. This time the figure was standing, his head bowed as though in prayer. On both occasions the figures were clearly defined, although the images disappeared after a few seconds.

A house named Bengal House in the town's Oxford Street was for some years during the 1960s and 1970s owned by the nearby White Hart Royal Hotel, being used as staff accommodation. Throughout this period occupants were troubled by inexplicable shuffling and giggling sounds that would often be heard during the night. Despite numerous attempts at finding the source, no cause was ever found. The problem was considered annoying rather than sinister, but it became such a persistent nuisance that several staff members refused to sleep in the building. Again a particular room was the scene for most of the paranormal activity, with lights switching on and off, and doors opening and closing apparently of their own accord. The house was sold many years ago, however, undergoing major alteration. There have been no further reports of strange activity.

There have, too, been a number of seemingly random incidences of haunting in the town. A house in Oxford Street was troubled by a poltergeist in the 1980s, with unaccounted-for footsteps and the banging of doors being regular annoyances. One room in particular was said to have a particularly unpleasant atmosphere, and it was finally decided to call upon the assistance of the clergy. An exorcism was conducted by a local minister, after which the difficulties ceased. One wonders whether the source of the trouble was actually a member of the household, rather than any unseen 'presence' in the building.

One of the Cornish Houses in Evenlode Road was a focus of poltergeist activity for a few weeks in the 1990s, with pictures throwing themselves off walls and electrical appliances turning themselves on and off. The peculiar activity stopped as suddenly as it had begun, though, and it is probably no coincidence that several children in the house had recently experienced domestic upheaval. Pond House in Parker's Lane is another dwelling that has had to endure the rather troublesome antics of a poltergeist, although as is often the case, the activity was fairly short-lived. Rapping sounds were heard, doors were banged sharply, and footsteps paced an upstairs landing. On one occasion a cup of tea was thrown across a room by some unseen entity. As recently as the early years of the twenty-first century properties in the town appeared to be home to 'residents' of unknown identity, and at Dereham Cottage in the High Street mysterious banging and creaking sounds were frequently heard. Unidentified voices were heard, too; then, in 2005, the apparition of a little boy wearing a gas mask was seen. Activities believed to emanate from 'beyond the grave' seem not confined to residential properties, either. A property situated opposite Moreton's war memorial in the High Street was, years ago, a shoe shop but has for decades been a restaurant. The building was once considered haunted, and several people on separate occasions in the late 1980s heard the distinct sound of a man clearing his throat in rooms where no one was present. Rather more of a nuisance, however, was a poltergeist that was active at the local pharmacy in the later years of the twentieth century. Eerie footsteps were heard pacing in an upstairs room, door handles were turned, as though by an unseen hand and neatly-stacked boxes were tossed about by some unseen force.

In the 1970s a tramp-like man was seen sitting at the edge of the town's horse pool, which is situated near The Inn on the Marsh – a public house beside the road to Stow-on-the-Wold. Moments after walking past the scruffy character, the witness turned to look at him and found that he had vanished. A local man is known to have drowned in the pool more than half a century earlier – was this his apparition?

One of Moreton's most

Moreton-in-Marsh Hospital.

enduring ghost stories is that of Miss Rebecca Horne and her white cats. The town's hospital was opened in 1873, and it was the conscientious and meticulous Miss Horne who was appointed its first Matron. If local superstition is to be believed, her attendance at the hospital has continued long into the afterlife, for stories of her ghostly figure being seen by modern-day nursing staff have been reported over many years. A number of nurses claim to have spotted her moving purposefully around in the building, and, indeed, it seems that almost any apparently inexplicable occurrence is put down to her ghostly presence. Almost inevitably, there have over the years been reports of eerie footsteps being heard in the wards and corridors; doors have apparently opened and closed of their own accord and an alarm used by staff to summon assistance has activated by itself.

Rather surprisingly – given the strict attention to cleanliness and discipline that would have prevailed in nineteenth-century hospitals – Miss Horne is said to have kept two white cats in the building. This claim seems to have been passed on through the generations, although whether it has any basis in truth must be a matter of some doubt. Various members of the hospital's nursing staff in the later years of the twentieth century have claimed that, when resting at night in an upstairs room, they felt the warm fur and plodding tread of these feline phantoms. One nurse even reported seeing a white cat in the room.

Apparently there have been long periods when Miss Horne and her cats have kept a very low profile. Now, in the twenty-first century, the building of a new hospital at another

Former aerodrome (Now the Fire Service College), Moreton-in-Marsh.

location is under way, and when healthcare activities are moved to the new facility it seems probable that the cats and their owner will remain in the building they know so well.

Prominent at the eastern edge of Moreton-in-Marsh is the town's internationally reputed Fire Service College, used for the training of Fire Service Officers. This facility stands on a well-preserved aerodrome that was used during the Second World War years for the training of Wellington bomber crews, and there are various ghost stories that originate from that time. After the end of the war the aerodrome became a Flying Training School, and what was known as the 'trolley acc' room was reputedly haunted. During the war, an aircraft had taken off with a WAAF passenger for a joy ride. The plane crashed into the 'trolley acc' room, however, and both the pilot and the WAAF passenger were killed. When the room was subsequently rebuilt there were endless equipment problems there, and RAF personnel claimed to have seen the WAAF girl.

An extraordinary story concerning what may have been a ghost aircraft has been related by a man who, in the late 1980s, was parked at the edge of the former aerodrome one night with a female companion. The couple suddenly found their quiet time together disturbed by the roar of what sounded like an aircraft engine and, looking out, the man saw a large plane coming towards him in the moonlight. It appeared to be an old-fashioned machine and was so low that the man dived down in the car. The mysterious plane passed overhead, however, and within a short time a very loud bang was heard, followed by silence. The man was convinced the plane must have crashed, and getting out of the car was surprised to see no sign of an accident.

Suddenly, however, from a road nearby there came the sound of voices raised in excitement, and the man saw a group of cyclists heading towards him. As he stared at this incongruous scene he saw the group were all wearing RAF uniform and seemed completely unaware of his presence. The group of cyclists then passed straight through a tall wire fence that surrounds the former aerodrome and continued until they were out of sight.

This fantastic account certainly raises several questions. Did the man – displaying remarkable powers of psychic perception – see a kind of apparitional 'recording'? And what could be the connection between the aircraft 'crash' and the group of phantom cyclists? It is unlikely that we will ever know and, although cynics might suspect hallucination caused by some unidentified factor, the detail presented is such that the account should not be dismissed as fantasy.

There are a few accounts of mysterious activities at the Fire Service College buildings, although these are confined to reports of vague poltergeist behaviour and one report of an apparition. When compared to the paranormal activity at the former aerodrome, however, these stories are relatively mundane.

When taken together, the accounts described above comprise a remarkable collection of folklore beliefs, legends, superstitions and accounts of paranormal and apparently inexplicable activity. Although most of the mysteries connected with Moreton-in-Marsh are related to stories of ghosts and incidences of haunting, other strange events have been reported, including several accounts of UFO sightings.

A credible witness has described how, in the early 1980s, he was standing on the London Road railway bridge in the town one evening, awaiting a train's arrival from Oxford. Dusk had fallen and he suddenly saw a strange sphere-shaped orange light hovering in the sky some distance away – more or less above the village of Evenlode. The light remained stationary in the sky for several minutes before suddenly hurtling away across the sky at incredible speed and vanishing from sight. The witness – a practical man and former member of an RAF aircrew – was certain that no conventional craft could have accelerated away at such speed and, although sceptical about the reliability of many UFO reports, was at a loss as to what this curious light was.

The 1950s and 1960s proved a fertile period throughout the country for reports of flying saucers. In this regard the alleged sighting by a local woman, who claimed that in the early 1950s she saw such a craft from her garden in Redesdale Place, was not quite as exceptional as might have been expected. It was a clear evening at the time and, according to the account given, a flying saucer suddenly appeared in the sky and hovered above a house nearby. A saucer-shaped craft with a dome on its upper side, it glowed orange, its edges lit by bright yellow light. The woman stated that the flying saucer was 'bigger than a house' and seemed to be little more than a 100ft above the ground. It was seen, apparently, by at least two other people, then, after hovering for several minutes, it rose up and shot off towards Stow-on-the-Wold.

There has been one more-recent report of a possible UFO. In the early years of the twenty-first century two women saw a peculiar object in the sky above Hospital Road one evening. They had gone out from their workplace at a residential care home into the darkness for a 'smoke break' when a bright white light suddenly came across the sky and hovered above them. The light, which was high in the sky like an aeroplane, was clearly defined, quite unlike a star, and was unaccompanied by sound. The light hovered for about five minutes, then, when one of the ladies went indoors and put on a light, it shot off at breakneck speed across the sky – much faster than could have been achieved by an aeroplane or helicopter. The size of the object was difficult to estimate, but it was large, bright and totally unlike the distant light of a star, planet or conventional aircraft.

In addition to years of ghostly manifestations and flying saucers, Moreton apparently attracted the attention of a black panther one day in 2006. Local newspaper, *The Gloucestershire Echo,* reported how a disabled woman on a mobility scooter was in the hospital car park when she came 'face-to-face' with a large black cat that was 'three to four yards away' in an adjacent field. Described as 'large and black, just like a panther', the beast looked as though it was going to pounce on something in the grass, when it spotted the woman and began to run towards her.

Fearing that the animal may attack her, the woman made good her escape. It seems that the 'panther' was less than interested, however, for it did not pursue the woman. It is probable that this is a case of mistaken identity, and that the 'panther' was actually a domestic cat, although this cannot be certain. If only it had been white it might have been judged one of the former matron's ghost-cats!

NAILSWORTH

Many years ago an inn called The Weavers' Arms was situated on a hill that leads from the old Bristol Road to Arnolds Lane at Nailsworth. It is said that a traveller was robbed and murdered there and that his ghost haunted the place thereafter, although most of the building was demolished in the late nineteenth century, and it is not thought that any incidences of haunting continue in the area nowadays.

Probably unconnected with ghosts and incidences of haunting, some curious moving lights were seen late one night in the summer of 2005 by a man who was watching a plane pass overhead. A very bright light suddenly appeared some distance from the plane, although there was no sound and it vanished as abruptly as it had appeared. This might have been forgotten, but a few evenings later the light was seen again and then, as it travelled across the sky, it split into two and travelled in two different directions. This was followed by three flashes of very bright intensity. The man went on to see about twenty similar UFOs during the course of a week leading him to speculate that perhaps some military testing had taken place.

According to legend, Nailsworth has its own black 'devil dog', similar to that seen elsewhere in Gloucestershire. This type of dog is popularly known by the name of 'Black Shuck' and, years ago, it was said that people walking along the road from Nailsworth to Horsley would sometimes see a black dog walking beside them, although it would vanish before Horsley was reached. This apparitional animal never showed any aggressive tendency, however, so the 'devil dog' epithet often ascribed to it seems rather harsh.

Naunton

On at least two occasions a mysterious figure in white has been seen at the Stow-on-the-Wold to Cheltenham road close to Naunton village. In 1998 an anaesthetist employed at Cheltenham General Hospital was driving along the road late one evening when a woman dressed in white smiled and waved at him as he drove towards her. Thinking she might need help, he stopped his car – only to find that she had vanished.

A couple of years later, in the spring of 2000, a man driving along the same road similarly late in the evening was startled when a white figure suddenly materialised in front of his car. There was no opportunity to take avoiding action and, although there was no apparent impact, the man screeched to a halt, fearing the worst. There was, however, no trace of the figure – though the man was so concerned that he reported the incident to the police. The origin of this ghostly apparition is unknown, but almost inevitably the spectre has acquired the nickname of 'The White Lady'.

NEWENT

There are a few reports of mysterious activity in the town of Newent. The figure of a man wearing a long dark coat has been seen trying to wave down cars travelling on the road to Kilcot. This spectral activity, which occurs most commonly near Crookes Farm just beyond the town, has apparently been the cause of at least one traffic accident. Early in the twentieth century a phantom Cavalier was supposed to have been seen wandering through the wall of a bedroom at The Old Court House. This apparition was seen to throw a cloak over one shoulder before disappearing from view.

Another place that boasts a resident ghost is the town's Tudor Fish and Chip Shop. This shop claims to have been serving up deep-fried delicacies since 1902, and apparently has a mysterious bearded ghost that appears behind the counter, wearing a black hat. This apparition has been seen by customers, at least one of whom assumed the figure to be an employee until advised otherwise by a staff member. Minor poltergeist activity has occurred at the shop, too, and stories that a person was killed on the site years ago have lead some to draw a connection.

An interesting tale of murder and ghostly activity is centred on remnants of the disused Hereford and Gloucester Canal, which can be seen near the town. Construction of this waterway commenced at Over, just outside Gloucester, in 1793 and by the late 1850s it had reached its commercial peak. It was during this time of relative prosperity that two Newent men bought a barge and began a lucrative business transporting materials from Gloucester to the farms of Newent. One of the men sought to gain complete control of the business, however, and murdered his colleague, weighing down the body and concealing it in the canal tunnel at Oxenhall – completed in 1798 – to the north-west of the town. Justice subsequently came about, though, and the body was discovered and the murderer hanged at Gloucester. The arrival of the railways saw to it that the days of the canal were numbered,

The Tudor Fish and Chip Shop, Newent.

Section of disused Hereford and Gloucester Canal,
Newent.

and it finally closed in 1881. It is claimed that to this day a ghostly barge is sometimes seen drifting eerily along the disused canal.

Newent's unusual occurrences are not confined to incidences of haunting and ghostly manifestations. In the summer of 1996 a number of reports of UFOs being seen throughout Gloucestershire were received. A small orange oval, about 700ft above the ground, caused particular interest when it was observed moving in a peculiar left to right sweeping motion in the sky between Newent and Upleadon.

The mid-1990s seem to have been a good period for peculiar activity in this part of Gloucestershire. In the summer of 1995 a doctor answering an emergency call at around the time dawn was breaking spotted a feline beast as it crossed the road in front of his car near Newent. Said to look somewhat like a puma, the animal was described as 'larger than a domestic cat, possibly 3ft or 4ft from nose to the tip of its long tail'. A slightly smaller, but otherwise identical, animal was seen one afternoon a couple of weeks later by a woman on the same stretch of road.

NEWLAND

Newland's splendid All Saints' Church is known as 'the Cathedral of the Forest' owing to its imposing size, and the entire village has a nicely-kept, peaceful feel to it. If legends and yarns are to be believed, however, the place is sometimes a hotbed of paranormal activity.

Cavaliers from the Civil War period are said to have been seen in and around the village. The Ostrich Inn is an excellent hostelry in the centre of Newland and, understandably, the Cavaliers are said to pay regular visits. The owners have yet to see them, though, so these apparitional figures are either very good at blending in with the earthly clientele or are only observed by people with especially perceptive abilities.

A ghostly coach has been seen careering through the village; from the window above a beautiful lady looks out anxiously at the passing scene. There is no record of any of these apparitions having been seen in recent times, however, and it is thought that they can safely be placed in the 'folklore and local tradition' category.

NORTH CERNEY

Among the most fascinating features of North Cerney are the remains of the Celtic tribal capital of the Belgic Dobunni, who inhabited much of Gloucestershire in the Iron Age. The most substantial evidence of the capital, in the form of a system of ramparts and ditches, is less than a mile south at the village of Bagendon, although earthworks near to North Cerney's Scrubditch Farm are certainly impressive.

More modern than the earthworks, but nevertheless of interest to anyone seeking evidence of the 'mysterious', is the village's twelfth-century church. On the outer south wall below the transept window the figure of a manticore has been scratched into the stone. This is thought to be a form of medieval graffiti left by the original masons. A manticore is a mythical creature with the body of a lion, a human head with rows of sharp teeth, porcupine quills, and the tail of a dragon or sting of a scorpion. In his book *Strange Britain*, Charles Walker states that manticores are '…said to be the demonic reversal of the four beasts which make up the four fixed signs of the zodiac – the lion of Leo, the human head of Aquarius and the scorpion of Scorpio, with the wings of the eagle turned into the featherless quills of a porcupine…'.

NORTH NIBLEY

According to local tradition, four spectral monks are sometimes seen in fields near Cotswold House to the west of North Nibley. The ghostly monks are said to carry a large wooden box or coffin on their shoulders, although it is claimed to contain treasure rather than a body. Legend has it that if anyone follows the monks to their destination a horde of buried treasure will be found. Unsurprisingly, no one has yet been able to follow the monks or find their treasure.

What is said to be the last battle fought between private armies on English soil took place at Nibley Green in 1469, and local tradition claims that a ghostly re-enactment of the battle is still heard occasionally. The families of Lord Berkeley of Berkeley Castle and Lord Lisle of Wotton had for generations disputed the rightful ownership of the Berkeley lands, and there had been several inconclusive skirmishes. On 19 March 1469, Thomas Talbot, the Viscount de Lisle, challenged Lord William Berkeley to combat on Nibley Green, near the village of North Nibley.

William accepted the challenge, enlisted support, and camped with his army that night on the outskirts of Michaelwood, next to Nibley Green.

Lord Lisle's army moved downhill to the green from North Nibley church at dawn on the following morning, and battle ensued. The battle was short, but very bloody, and Berkeley's army quickly established superiority. Lord Lisle was shot with an arrow in the eye and then killed with a dagger; his army were routed.

It is said that on 19 March of each year the sounds of marching troops and horses can be heard close to the spot where Lord William encamped, and that on the battlefield at Nibley Green the sounds of battle – flying arrows, clashing swords, galloping horses' hooves, and the awful sounds made by the wounded and dying – can still be heard.

Paranormal activity of a different nature has, allegedly been witnessed by a licensee at the village's Black Horse Inn. Several ghostly figures are claimed to have been seen, including two that are thought to be the apparitions of former licensees. There have been incidents involving poltergeist activity, including frequent inexplicable banging sounds coming from a loft. In 2007, a team of researchers into the supernatural carried out an investigation at the inn and are said to have found much evidence of paranormal activity.

NORTHLEACH

Like a number of towns in the county, Northleach is supposed to have several secret tunnels and passages running beneath it, and an incident in 1937 lent credibility to some of the legends. A young woman was pushing a small child in a pram at the West End area of the town when the ground of the garden path at Guggle Cottage suddenly gave way beneath her feet. She began to fall into a hole and was saved only by the quick reactions of her boyfriend, who pulled her out.

An underground tunnel some 40ft deep was revealed, beyond which was a room with barrel vaulting. This curious structure, which was estimated to date from the fourteenth century, had several tunnels radiating out from it, and local people are said to have followed them – although not to their full extent. It seems highly probable, however, that the tunnels led under the main road. There has long been a tradition that stone for the church was quarried in the centre of Northleach, and apparently the tunnels and walls showed evidence of tooling. It has been claimed that one of the tunnels ran to the church and that, during the Civil War period, treasures from the church were hidden in the tunnels. There is no evidence to support this claim, however, and it seems more likely

'Green Man' at Northleach Church.

that the 'room' and tunnels were actually remnants of an ancient quarry. Unfortunately, it will never be known how far the tunnels really extended, for the ancient remains were filled-in soon after being exposed.

Another of the town's secret tunnels is supposed to lead from The Red Lion Inn – parts of which are estimated to date from the fourteenth century – and across the market square opposite, and this is supposed to have been explored many years ago. Apparently it was followed for more than 200ft until it was discovered that a collapse prevented further exploration. This tunnel, too, was said to be heading towards the town's Church of St Peter and St Paul. This splendid building, which is certainly worth exploration, has its own little mystery in the form of a 'green man', which can be seen on a corbel in the porch.

For a town with so many ancient hiding places, there are very few tales of incidences of haunting and apparitions, although a couple of the public houses are said to have resident ghosts. The apparition of an old man holding his hands to his head has on several occasions been seen sitting at a table in a corner of the bar at The Red Lion Inn, while various apparently inexplicable noises and minor activities at The Sherborne Arms are attributed to a long-since deceased character nicknamed 'Long Fred'.

OWLPEN

Nestling in a woodland hollow, the beautiful village of Owlpen is formed by a picturesque group of buildings that includes a church, a mill and the lovely fifteenth-century Owlpen Manor – reputedly haunted by several ghosts.

Most illustrious of the supernatural residents is the ghost of Queen Margaret, wife of King Henry VI. She and her son, Prince Edward, are thought to have stayed at Owlpen Manor in 1471, and the house was subsequently said by Margaret to have been the place where she spent her last happy night, before the murder of Edward at the Battle of Tewkesbury a couple of days later.

A number of people claim to have seen the apparition of a 'grey lady' in fifteenth-century garb, and it has been assumed to be the ghost of Queen Margaret. Roy Palmer, in his book *Folklore of Gloucestershire*, describes how in 1943 a young evacuee saw '…a lady wearing a dress with tight bodice, baggy shoulders and long, tapering sleeves, together with a high steeple hat with lace down the back, and pointed shoes…' As recently as 1991, apparently, a visitor sleeping in Queen Margaret's room awoke and saw a phantom female figure bending over a writing table.

Queen Margaret's ghost is said to be completely benign, but another presence at Owlpen Manor has been less willingly accepted. Thought to be the ghost of an alchemist, this entity is said to have 'slapped' a boy staying at the house, causing him shock and

Owlpen Manor, Owlpen.

distress. An exorcism was subsequently held, the end result apparently being a considerable 'lightening' of the atmosphere there.

Finally, a hooded figure known as 'The Black Monk' has reportedly been seen prowling around in the east wing of the house. Various rather doubtful suggestions as to the figure's identity have been made, perhaps the most interesting being that he had fled Kingswood Abbey at nearby Wotton-under-Edge during the Reformation, then been bricked into a 'hidden room' at Owlpen Manor. The room seems to have been rather too well hidden, however, for no exit was provided and, years later, his skeleton was said to have been found during alterations.

OZLEWORTH

A handsome former hunting lodge named Newark Park, built around 1550 by Sir Nicholas Poyntz, can be visited at the pretty village of Ozleworth. Poyntz lived near Bristol and wanted a restful place where he and his guests could stay after a day's hunting, so he created the Lodge using stone from Kingswood Abbey. The abbey, situated a little to the south-west of Wotton-under-Edge, had been destroyed during King Henry VIII's Dissolution of the Monasteries.

It is said that monks trying to flee the abbey became trapped in a subterranean passage, their skeletons being discovered years later. Tradition has it that when the stone from the

Newark park, Ozleworth.

abbey was taken to Newark Park, the monks' spirits came with it. Their phantoms were subsequently seen coming from a panelled wall, across a room and down a staircase – solemnly chanting as they went. Whether their restless ghosts can still be seen is a matter for conjecture, but the house is now in the care of the National Trust, so may be visited by the general public.

PaiNSWiCk

This village seems to have more paranormal and mysterious aspects to it than might be expected. First there is an apparitional thatcher, complete with smock and wide-brimmed hat, who is said to appear from time to time in various parts of Painswick. His visits are confined to those fairly rare occasions when thatching is actually taking place at some building in the village, when he is said to have been witnessed standing in the road or garden below, gazing up at the craftsmanship taking place above.

A rather more notable apparition, in the form of a ghostly Cavalier – thought to be that of King Charles I himself – has been seen ambling around Painswick's Court House in Hale Lane, as have various other figures claimed to be 'Cavaliers'. All of these phantoms are said to date from when King Charles and members of his army were based at the Court House during the siege of Gloucester in 1643.

A large Edwardian house named Gyde House, situated in Gyde Lane, was the subject of an article in *The Daily Telegraph* in 2001, when the place was being converted into apartments by property developers. Gyde House was named after nineteenth-century philanthropist Edwin Francis Gyde and operated as an orphanage between 1920 and 1997, during which period many youngsters knew it as home. According to most accounts, the orphanage was a happy, well-run place and there seems little evidence of anything particularly untoward having happened there. Even so, the site manager for the company who undertook the conversion reported that the house had a terrible feeling about it and that children's voices were inexplicably heard echoing about the place. He put all this down to his suspicion that some children had been abused in the old shower blocks.

Finally a local psychic and faith healer was called in to try and solve the problem. She was told that three children had hanged themselves from trees on the northern edge of the property, and she then set about blessing them and praying for them – a procedure that apparently left her 'absolutely exhausted' and hardly able to breathe. This activity had the desired result, it seems, for there have been no reports of problems since.

'Black Shuck', Gloucestershire's legendary 'hell hound', comes nearer to the village then many might wish, having been seen – according to folklore – in company with an ugly goblin at Stepping Stone Lane. This spectral pair are said to appear close to a milestone marked '7 miles to Gloster', which is situated beside this old coach road that runs between Painswick and Stroud.

Considerably more lifelike than the illusive 'Black Shuck' was a big cat that was reportedly seen in Painswick's Lower Washwell Street in the summer of 2004. A man

Gyde House, Painswick.

walking there in the evening spotted the animal walking about twenty yards ahead of him. Pitch black in colour, it was described as 'about twenty inches high at the shoulder', with 'narrow hips and a long tail of uniform roundness along its entire length'. Displaying considerable bravery (or recklessness), the man whistled at the beast to encourage it to turn around and, as if to oblige, it turned to face him and revealed 'the short face, yellow eyes and small ears of a classic panther profile'. A car then passed and it ambled across the street, before jumping a 5½ft high fence and disappearing from view.

PARKEND

Once a thriving coal mining centre, Parkend is nowadays a peaceful village surrounded by woodlands. Although there may well be a tale or two of ghosts in and around the village, none has yet come to light, and it is the woodland and its inhabitants that present the most interesting mystery.

Through the first few years of the twenty-first century hundreds of reports of big cat sightings were made to the Gloucestershire Constabulary and, while many people are likely to have merely seen large domestic cats, it seems unrealistic to assume every report to have been a case of 'mistaken identity'. Lydney-based big cat expert, Danny Nineham, is convinced that leopards are present in the Forest of Dean, and that the extent of the problem is being concealed by the authorities. There are reasonable explanations regarding the possible presence of such animals in the UK. Some may be the result of escaped zoo or circus animals, but more likely is a large release of captive species that probably took place when the Dangerous Wild Animals Act was enforced in the 1970s.

the Forest of Dean has long been considered a likely haven for big cats, with reported sightings in the first five years of the twenty-first century lending particular credibility to the idea. Following a Freedom of Information Act request, the Forestry Commission revealed that rangers taking part in a deer survey and using thermal imaging cameras spotted what were thought to be big cats on two separate occasions in the Forest of Dean. Both sightings were considered reliable and were made at night, using heat-activated night vision equipment. The first sighting was at the edge of Churchill enclosure east of Parkend in February 2002 and the second was on the southern slopes of Staple Edge, near Soudley, in March 2005, the thermal cameras showed a large feline, which could not be explained. Mark Robson, the Gloucestershire Constabulary's Wildlife and Environmental Crime Officer, said that he considered the Forestry Commission's evidence to be credible.

POULTON

A crossroads just outside the village has long been known as Betty's Grave, although precisely who 'Betty' was is something of a mystery. There are various stories about her and why she ended up at the crossroads. Some say she was a gypsy woman who was murdered and buried at the spot; another story is that she was actually named 'Betty Bastoe' and was buried at the crossroads when, in 1786, she dropped dead after winning a bet that she could cut an acre of wheat in record time. If this yarn seems unlikely, then other accounts are only marginally more believable: she was a witch who was burned and buried there; she was hanged for sheep-stealing; she was a suicide who could not be buried in consecrated ground; she was poisoned by her employer or she, in fact, poisoned her employer.

Katharine Briggs, in her book *The Folklore of the Cotswolds*, describes how Poulton residents once believed that witches at the crossroads '…used to

Betty's Grave, Poulton.

amuse themselves by holding up the pedlars on their way to Fairford market…' and would use their magic to keep them there all day, unable to move. It is said that the area around the grave is to this day haunted by Betty and, quite possibly, the other witches as well. It will, of course, never be known for sure which version of events is true, but it is likely that the folklore surrounding Betty and her grave will live on for many years.

PRESTBURY

This little village stands close to the edge of Cheltenham's famous racecourse, and has nowadays been almost absorbed into the outskirts of the town. It has managed to retain its own identity, however, and is reputed to be the most haunted village in Gloucestershire. Other locations, such as Painswick, might be inclined to contest this, and there are certainly several small towns, such as Moreton-in-Marsh, that can claim to have a similar number of ghosts and folklore traditions. None, though, has any that sounds quite as ominous and evocative as Prestbury's 'Black Abbot'.

The black abbot is, apparently, seen quite often in the vicinity of the church, and his hooded figure has been reported walking from the church towards Reform Cottage (which used to be a tithe barn from which, it is said, a secret passage leads to the church). His footsteps have been heard approaching the cottage, then, moments later, were heard pacing around in an attic, followed by disruptive crashing and banging sounds, as though the place were being turned upside down. Subsequent investigation revealed nothing untoward in the attic, however. The abbot is said to appear most frequently at Easter, on All Saints' Day and at Christmas, but for those unwilling to wait for his appearance, a picture purporting to be his photograph can be seen hanging in the bar of Prestbury's Royal Oak pub.

Horsemen, too, feature prominently among Prestbury's ghost stories. A phantom rider has supposedly been seen on a white horse galloping through Shaw Green Lane and The Burgage as recently as 1989. This apparition is said to be the ghost of a horseman who was killed by a Lancastrian arrow, allegedly on 4 May 1471, when on his way to Tewkesbury during the Wars of the Roses. His earthly remains are thought to have been discovered in 1901 when part of a skeleton – with an arrow in its ribs – was discovered during repairs to the lane at Shaw Green.

Another of Prestbury's well-known ghost stories is that of a phantom Cavalier on horseback, who has been heard, many times, galloping through The Burgage and Mill Lane. He has been heard at other places in the village, too, including Bowbridge Lane and Shaw Green Lane. It is said that when the hoof-beats are heard in the road known as The Burgage, they come to a very abrupt stop. The Cavalier is the ghost of a Royalist messenger, apparently, who was brought off his horse by Parliamentarian sympathisers in Prestbury, who had stretched a rope across the road in his path. The rope caught him under the chin, according to the popular story, and when he was unseated he was swiftly killed and buried nearby.

Again in the same area, paranormal activity of an audible nature occurred when, years ago, a man walking his dog in Mill Lane one foggy evening heard the distinctive sound of a number of men marching towards him through the fog. His dog apparently sensed the activity, too, for it became uneasy and sank down on its haunches. The sound stopped as abruptly as it had started, however, and no figures appeared. This appears not to have been a totally isolated incident, however, and another, similar report was subsequently received.

The Royal Oak public house is situated near the scene of Prestbury's ghostly horse-riders. Indeed, an apparitional equestrian from more modern times was allegedly seen by a group of four women on the day of one of Cheltenham's famous Gold Cup race meetings in the 1970s. The women saw a man in jockey's clothing at the kerbside nearby, then, as he began to cross the road, he vanished before reaching the other side. As if by magic, he was seen again a short while later, this time crossing

Prestbury Church.

the road around the corner. Whether this really was paranormal activity may be open to some doubt, particularly as it occurred outside a pub on a busy race day.

Numerous other locations in the village are said to be haunted. Sundial Cottage, also in The Burgage, is supposed to be home to a rather musical ghost. Towards the end of the nineteenth century a music professor gave lessons at the cottage, and the ethereal sound of a spinet (a small type of piano or harpsichord) being played has been heard – although not since the 1940s. The apparition of a young girl in a summer dress was seen in the garden at around the period that the professor was giving his music lessons, so whether the ghostly music was being played by the girl or her teacher must be a matter for guesswork.

The grounds of the nearby Prestbury House Hotel are claimed by some to be haunted by the apparition of a nineteenth-century servant girl named 'Lizzie', who used to wait on patrons attending there when it was a tea room catering to the needs of crowds attending the nearby Cheltenham racecourse. 'Lizzie' has been seen walking in the wooded grounds of the hotel, wearing a long dress and a small cap of white cloth on her head.

A converted coach-house named Walnut Cottage can be found in Tatchley Lane. This is said to be haunted by a character known as 'Old Moses' – a long-deceased local resident who used to carry out odd jobs in the village. This elderly ghost was fond of suddenly appearing in the dining room, according to history, and once when a visitor to the cottage encountered him standing by a fireplace, announced 'Here's Old Moses! You see I likes to look in sometimes.'

The owner of the property refused to believe in the existence of ghosts, and one day sat down for dinner at the dining table, loudly proclaiming as much. As if in response, a large mirror promptly fell off the wall. It is not known whether Old Moses made regular appearances, or whether the legend is in fact rather more substantial than the alleged haunting that inspired it. The last recorded sighting of the apparition was in 1961.

Many other paranormal events and folklore traditions in Prestbury seem, in the main, to be somewhat vague or are relatively insignificant. The road outside The Plough Inn at Mill Street has long had a reputation for possessing some kind of atmosphere or presence that affects animals. Herdsmen would often encounter difficulty in getting their sheep to pass the location; horses would be reluctant to walk the road; and dogs would become restless and apparently rooted to the spot. A local postman often used to hear the sound of horses' hooves behind him near the inn, and would move over to allow them to pass. No horse ever passed, however, the sound suddenly stopping and no animal appearing. It is said that a misty white form has sometimes been seen gliding over fields next to the lane and this has always been known as 'Mrs Preece's ghost'. No one seems to know who this lady was or when 'she' was last seen.

A ghostly flock of sheep, accompanied by a shepherd in nineteenth-century rural dress, is said to have been seen in Prestbury's Swindon Lane, and a funeral procession with black horses and mourners dressed in black was seen crossing a field next to Southam Road by a teacher returning by car to Cheltenham. Puzzled, the teacher turned the car around so that she could look again at the unusual procession. There was, however, no sign of it and it was assumed that the mourners and horses were apparitional.

Prestbury's High Street has not been without paranormal activity. There have long been rumours of ghostly activity at The King's Arms public house, with several staff members apparently having seen apparitions or experienced minor poltergeist activity. The apparition of an old lady in medieval clothing is said to have been seen window shopping along the street, and at least two of the business premises experienced poltergeist activity years ago. None of the ghosts and apparitions described seem in any way malevolent, but the village does have one hostile presence. A seventeenth-century house named Cleeve Corner, close to the church, is supposed to have been the site of a murder at some indeterminate point in the dim and distant past. The story goes that a young bride was strangled by a burglar who made off with her wedding gifts and valuables. What became of the murderer is not known, but it is claimed that an evil presence haunts the room in which the wicked act took place. It is claimed that visitors staying there are awoken in the night by an unearthly light that shines through the window. The temperature drops and an awful pressure is felt on the throat as the spectral strangler – for surely it must be he? – seeks to re-enact his murderous assault. The pressure grows tighter and tighter, being released only when the victim coughs out a prayer. Mercifully, there have been no incidents involving strangulation at the house within living memory, so it may be assumed that potential victims have all been devout and quick-thinking.

It seems likely that Prestbury's reputation as one of the most haunted villages in England will remain secure. It is even said that a ley line joins the village with other famously reputedly haunted locations in Gloucestershire, namely The Ram Inn at Wotton-under-Edge and Woodchester Mansion.

RANDWICK

E.P. Fennemore, in an antiquated publication named *History of Randwick*, stated that in 1892 the village '…has always been a fertile field for ghost-lore, and many are the ghost tales on record. Many houses also in years gone by have been "haunted" – notably, two well known to the writer…'

Fennemore goes on to mention a tradition that an underground passage runs from Randwick Church to an Elizabethan manor house named Moor Hall, about a quarter of a mile to the south-east. A Stonehouse man named White, apparently, 'kept company' with a Miss Pegler of Moor Hall, their names being inscribed on a window of the house. After consultation with a witch, White was told he would go on to commit suicide by hanging, after committing an offence 'worthy of this punishment'.

The witch's prediction came true and White duly hanged himself, a 'tremendous thunderstorm' occurring at the burial. This was considered a judgement upon White, whose ghost was – according to tradition – subsequently 'laid' in the middle of the churchyard.

For years there have been vague stories of the woods above Randwick being haunted. Claims have been made that a galloping horse has been heard, and yet not seen – even though it passed right by the witness. Another story tells of Randwick woods being haunted by a ghostly monk whose photograph could at one time be seen at The Vine Tree public house in the village.

REDBROOK

This pretty village in the Wye Valley is very close to the border with Monmouthshire, in Wales. It was once a thriving industrial centre, largely due to a good water supply that ran down the valley and surrounding hills into the River Wye. From Swan Pool, a number of dams and reservoir ponds were created, with industrial sites including mills, an iron furnace, tinplate works and copper works.

Swan Pool, situated close to the minor road that runs to Newland, has long been reputed to be haunted by the figure of a tall woman in white, with a crying baby in her arms. The ghost has only appeared at night, when her figure – draped in weeds and dripping with water – has been seen to rise slowly from the dark water of the pool. After her appearance a large black 'hell-hound' emerges from the ruins of an old lime kiln in the nearby woods, walks down to the pool, then walks around it once before returning to its lair in the lime kiln.

Tradition has it that the woman either murdered her baby, or that both – and possibly the dog as well – were murder victims. Rupert Matthews, in his book *Haunted Gloucestershire*, says that the figure is the ghost of a local teenage girl who in the eighteenth century became pregnant by a wealthy married farmer from Newland. It seems that the man's method of dealing with the dilemma was to murder his lover, because her battered body was subsequently found in Swan Pool. He was proved responsible, apparently, and was hanged for the crime. Whether this account has any factual basis is not known.

REDMARLEY D'ABITOT

This village, which has close borders with Herefordshire and Worcestershire, takes its curious name from the D'Abitot family who held the manor from the late twelfth century until the first quarter of the fourteenth century.

Accounts of mysteries in the village seem sparse, but in 1994 a man driving down a minor road near Redmarley saw a huge black cat cross in front of his headlights one evening. The animal was described as 'grey or black with a tail which came straight down and then curled back up at the end'. Some years later, in the summer of 2008, the area made it to the local press after a motorist reported seeing a big cat when it dashed out in front of his car. He had been driving along the A417 road near the junction with the M50 late one July evening when he narrowly missed hitting the animal, which he described as about 2ft in height, and jet black with a curled tail. There was no doubt in his mind that what he had seen was a black panther.

He was shocked by the incident, so pulled in at the nearby Rose and Crown public house at Redmarley and described what he had seen. A man there said that such sightings 'happened all the time' and that a pair of panthers roamed the area. A local farmer, apparently, frequently complained about the animals killing his sheep. It seems that the 'beasts of Gloucestershire' are alive and well and may be living in the area around Redmarley.

RODBOROUGH

The apparition of a coach and horses, with a figure wearing a tall hat and standing on the back of the carriage, is reported to have been seen descending the steep hill from Rodborough Common towards Woodchester in the valley below. The apparition was seen in the early 1970s approaching the driveway to Rodborough Manor, and was seen again in 1977, this time by a couple of teenagers. It is now more than thirty years since a reported sighting, however, so it may be that the coach has reached its final destination.

Close to the top of Walkley Hill on the Rodborough and Minchinhampton road out of Stroud is a convivial and attractive public house named The Prince Albert. At the back of the building is a courtyard where several people have reported what seems to have been the apparition of an American GI soldier.

Also on Walkley Hill is a road named Rectory Close. The apparition of a young woman in a long, grey dress has been seen a number of times walking to or from a property known as Jarolen House. Apparently paying no attention to vehicles and people, the woman is thought to be the ghost of a maid who worked at the house in the nineteenth century.

RUARDEAN

It will come as no surprise, given its coal-mining past, that the Forest of Dean is supposed to be haunted by numerous miners. The desperate cries of one such character are said to be heard on certain nights coming from the Pan Tod mine at the top of Ruardean Hill. The cries are believed to be those of a particularly mean-spirited mine owner who, years ago, quarrelled with his men at the top of the mine shaft. Whether he fell or was pushed is not known, but it was at the bottom of the mine that he ended up. And that is where he stayed, apparently, until years later a pile of rags and bones found in the mine were identified as his. The Pan Tod mine was closed many years ago and nothing now remains of it, although a Mining Memorial Topograph – created in memory of five local miners who lost their lives in the mines – was erected at the top of Ruardean Hill in 2008.

Miners' Memorial Topograph, Ruardean Hill.

Ruardean is probably as well known for its beasts as for its ghosts. A fine carving of Saint George fighting the mythical dragon can be seen above the door of the church, and stories of panther-like beasts in the forest are far from uncommon. Wild boar, too, are known to frequent the woods, but the story of the forest's bear-killers is perhaps the area's most enduring legend.

Many people in Gloucestershire and its neighbouring counties have only a vague idea of what actually took place, so the facts of the incident are outlined here. The year was 1889 and four Frenchmen were travelling in the district with two performing Russian black bears. The animals were chained and muzzled and had been trained for some months.

The men and their bears first went to Ruardean, where a dancing display was performed to the amusement of onlookers, who readily gave a few coppers to the Frenchmen. They then proceeded to Cinderford, three miles away, where the bears performed dancing displays in various parts of the town. Following this, the Frenchmen and their animals made their way back towards Ruardean, intending to give further displays at several villages in the area. Many of Cinderford's children were excitedly following in a procession behind the men and bears.

When the bears got to the foot of Ruardean, however, the children had been joined by a number of angry men who had been drinking in nearby public houses. A malicious and totally untrue rumour began to circulate, that the bears had killed a woman in Cinderford. It was also said a woman had been mauled so severely that she would be scarred for life. Soon the mood became ugly and the children ran back to Cinderford. The Frenchmen and their animals became surrounded by a mob of more than forty threatening men, and as they pressed on to Ruardean they were beaten and insulted along the way. Many more men had joined the baying mob by this time and the crowd eventually numbered around 200. Stones and makeshift weapons were used to attack the Frenchmen and bears, and as they reached the outskirts of Ruardean they became almost hysterical with fear and pain. The bears had broken loose from their chains and were ambling in bewildered fashion ahead of the mob, and one of the tormentors smashed a wooden pole onto the smaller bear's head. Covered with blood, dirt and steam, it sank down dead on the road. Two of the Frenchmen escaped into the woods, while another hid in a pig-sty until he was dragged out. The fourth Frenchman made good his escape, although it was not known where he went.

The larger bear carried on through Ruardean – being pelted with stones and beaten with clubs – until, when it got about a mile beyond the village, someone shot it and another man cut its throat. The police did not become involved until after the event, when an officer took two of the Frenchmen into his protection and had the dead bears stored in a barn. Thirteen men subsequently appeared before magistrates sitting at Littledean Police Court, charged with ill-treating, torturing and maliciously killing two bears and assaulting the Frenchmen. All but two of the men were found guilty and received very heavy fines. An appeal was subsequently launched for the Frenchmen and a substantial sum of money was raised.

The stain on the people of the Forest of Dean remained for many years, however. Indeed, to a very minor degree, an element of ridicule and contempt is still occasionally expressed.

It has been said for years that to ask anyone from Ruardean 'Who killed the bears?' was a sure way to attract a punch on the nose or, at the very least, a sharp retort. This is probably because the people of Ruardean were for years wrongly considered bear-killers. It was, in fact, a mob of men from Cinderford that was responsible for the killings, and Ruardean inhabitants witnessing the violence sheltered and nursed the injured Frenchmen.

What finally became of the dead bears is something of a mystery. It is claimed that one of the bodies, at least, was buried in the garden of the police station at Drybrook, although the accuracy of this is open to doubt. Others think the bears may have been buried in the police station garden at Ruardean. As no official record of the burials exists the subject is a matter for informed guesswork or future excavation.

RUSPIDGE

This parish to the south of Cinderford has in recent years come to the attention of those with an interest in alleged big cat sightings. Reports have been made of large animals being seen in the vicinity, with two apparent sightings taking place in 2006. A dog walker believed he came face to face with a leopard, and then a few months later two schoolboys ran for their lives when a large green-eyed animal crashed through the undergrowth nearby. In 2007 there were further sightings when, on separate occasions, a big cat was encountered by a milkman, a firefighter, and a lorry driver.

As recently as May 2010 two girls, aged fifteen and eight, reported seeing a black panther in woods near Ruspidge. The feline beast, which was at one point just five metres from the girls, was described as about the size of a Great Dane, black all over, with big eyes and paws, and a long tail. The older girl was quite definite that it was a big cat.

A subsequent feature in *The Daily Mail* included information from Forest of Dean-based big-cat enthusiast Danny Nineham, who stated his belief that the cat is a particularly large male black leopard, and a Gloucestershire Constabulary representative is on record as saying he believes a pair of big cats – probably panthers – to be living in the Forest of Dean.

ST BRIAVELS

This village, which stands high above the Rive Wye, has an interesting castle, much of which dates from the thirteenth century. The place has long been considered haunted by numerous ghosts, including a knight in armour, a lady in white, a crying baby and a man in centuries-old costume. The knight was seen in the castle grounds in the 1950s, apparently, while the inexplicable sound of a crying baby has been heard in the castle's solar room. It is said that during ceiling repairs to the room some years ago the wrapped corpse of a baby fell from the rafters. Additionally, a ghostly black dog has been reported as appearing on the floor between the chapel and the Great Hall, and a couple of amateur 'ghost hunters' staying at the castle in 2006 believed they witnessed a canine apparition.

Some believe there may be a secret tunnel running underground from the castle to the nearby George Inn. This old drinking establishment is said to be haunted, and there are claims that a ghostly Cavalier has been seen there. A phantom monk – nicknamed 'George' – is reportedly another regular visitor and has been seen by a number of the regular patrons.

It seems, too, that one of the infamous big cats of the Forest of Dean may have paid a visit to the village in 1997. A local resident was at home watching television one evening when he turned on the security lights at the rear of the house, revealing a large black creature attacking the dustbin. The animal froze as the light illuminated it, only running off when the resident banged on the glass of the window. It was described as '…about the size of an Alsatian dog with smooth black hair, but it was definitely cat-like…'.

St Briavels Castle.

SAINTBURY

The minor road that runs down through the village of Saintbury joins the Broadway to Mickleton road at the foot of the hill. Next to this junction is a village cross, the shaft of which may date from the fourteenth century, and it is here that funeral processions are believed to have rested before ascending the hill to the village church. This location also marks the first point of a significant ley line that runs across country for 3½ miles to Seven Wells, near Snowshill.

A leyline is a straight line that runs through a number of ancient sites. The idea that significant sites were often joined by 'leys' was first put forward by pioneer photographer and amateur archaeologist Alfred Watkins in his 1925 book *The Old Straight Track*. The suggestion that the alignment of such sites is no accident has always been somewhat contentious, and for every person who suggests mystical interpretations there is another who scoffs at the notion. Nevertheless, whether by accident or design, it is a fact that many ancient sites are aligned – and the 'Saintbury ley' is one such site.

From the cross at the foot of the hill, the ley passes through the Church of St Nicholas – an early Norman building with much of interest – in the village, then on through a Bronze-Age round barrow just above the church, to a Neolithic long barrow on Willersey Hill, a Saxon cemetery nearby (precise location not known) and finally to Seven Wells, near Spring Hill, which – according to Danny Sullivan in his book *Ley Lines* – is a place 'locally associated with medieval witchcraft'.

Incidentally, Saintbury's Church of St Nicholas has a number of Pagan symbols and over the door, almost hidden by a porch that has been added, there is a curious carving of a horned, devilish figure.

Sceptics might point to the fact that a number of the sites are of widely differing eras, and some may feel that, given a long ruler and a detailed map of the county, one might come up with any number of 'alignments'. Nevertheless, the subject is regarded with reverence by many, and in the 1970s, apparently, the 'Saintbury ley' was the subject of rigorous statistical analysis by a mathematician, who proved the line to be 'significant at the 1% level'. This, says writer Danny Sullivan, means that the alignment was 'probably deliberate'.

SAUL

There is little to see in this small village near the River Severn, and if there are any tales of ghosts and mysteries they have yet to come to light. However, a sighting in the village in 1997 of what may have been a big cat can be included in any debate about the mysterious 'beasts' that are believed to roam the area.

The witness was looking out of his bedroom window one morning when 'a huge black panther' was seen about five hundred yards away. The witness used binoculars to watch the animal for about five minutes, before it '...slunk off into the undergrowth.' A few months later three fishermen in the same area were returning home late in the evening when they observed something unusual crossing the road ahead of their car. One of the witnesses made the following comment: '…it was looking at us and its eyes were glowing red. We all got a very good view. It was black all over and it was a huge cat like a panther. It had a long tail which curved down to the ground and turned up again. It was long and thin and much too big for a dog.' This description does seem to indicate a panther or similar large feline, although glowing red eyes might more commonly be associated with 'hell-hounds' and spectral dogs.

SELSLEY

The church in this hillside village just outside Stroud was constructed in 1861-62 to a design by architect G.F. Bodley. It is of the French-Gothic style, with a somewhat incongruous saddleback tower, and interesting stained glass by William Morris and other leading figures of the Pre-Raphaelite circle. It has been suggested – notably, by researcher, Geoff Bird – that construction of the church followed principles of the gematria system. This Hebrew system, possibly derived from Greek geometry, assigns numerical value to an alphabet and is ostensibly a method of discovering hidden truths and meanings behind words. Bird claimed in an article in *Gloucestershire Earth Mysteries* magazine that certain measurements add up to specific values that equate to various supposed immortal figures, Jesus Christ and, indeed, the universe as a whole.

Confused? One might perhaps be forgiven for being completely baffled. Even so, the seeds of interest may have been sown for those enthused by the relationship between mathematics and ancient earth mysteries.

SHEEPSCOMBE

It is said that Anne Boleyn and King Henry VIII were fond of riding and hunting in the beech woods around Sheepscombe. According to tradition, Anne still wanders in Sheepscombe Woods, and it is said that her apparition has been seen, sometimes together with the smiling Henry VIII. There is no record of these ghosts having been seen within living memory, however, so it seems reasonable to regard this as ancient folklore. Another folklore account is of a lady in a long lavender dress, said to haunt the lane outside The Butchers Arms in Sheepscombe. When she was last seen is not known, although there are vague stories of a ghost having been seen in the pub's loft within the past few years.

SHERBORNE

The impressive Sherborne House, substantially rebuilt in the nineteenth century, stands close to Sherborne's small village church – the yard of which was apparently the scene of

Sherborne Churchyard.

a few flying American bullets in the years of the Second World War. American servicemen were billeted at the house during the war, and it soon became clear that a number of the men believed the place haunted.

A serviceman on guard duty one night thought that he saw a ghostly white spectre moving among the graves in the churchyard and, in true American spirit, let a shot loose from his rifle. Other servicemen came to the guard's assistance and a thorough search for the white figure was carried out. However, nothing was found, and it became accepted that the figure had indeed been a ghost. There is a story in the village that a 'ghost' was seen by a serviceman on a further occasion, and that this time when a shot was fired a fellow serviceman was hit – although not fatally. This account does have the ring of fantasy about it, although regular listeners to news bulletins will be aware that 'friendly fire' incidents are to this day far from rare.

SHIPTON OLIFFE

The oldest parts of The Frogmill Inn, which stands close to the old road between Gloucester and London, are claimed to date to the eleventh century. It has certainly been a coaching inn since the seventeenth century, although major alterations to the building took place in 1950 and more recently following the severe floods of 2007.

The oldest parts of the inn have long had the reputation of being haunted, with one room, in particular, apparently being a focus for paranormal activity. Apparitions including an old man, a child and a young girl have been seen, and unaccountable footsteps have been heard pacing about the place. Perhaps most alarming, however, is a dense mist that has supposedly been seen issuing from each corner of the room and meeting in the centre. The mist is sometimes accompanied by the sounds of whispering voices that seem to come from the ceiling. This tale relates to reports made many years ago, however, and although eerie footsteps are still heard occasionally the ghostly mist seems to have dissipated.

SLAD

Bull's Cross, on the road leading north-east out of the village, has an old folklore tradition attached to it in the form of a phantom stagecoach. Local resident Laurie Lee, in his famously evocative book *Cider with Rosie*, describes how the apparition of a fatal stagecoach crash is sometimes seen at midnight, particularly on New Year's Eve. The awful sight of the hopelessly out-of-control carriage and horses is accompanied by the sounds of screaming passengers and splintering wood.

Until his death in 1997, Laurie Lee was a regular visitor to The Woolpack Inn at Slad, and it is upon this fine hostelry that some paranormal activities – such as doors that apparently open of their own accord – are centred. One Robert John Bond, a former licensee at the inn, committed suicide there in 1898 by cutting his throat, and it is thought that perhaps the inexplicable occurrences are connected with this unfortunate event.

SLING

Standing among the trees on Clearwell Meend by the side of the road from Coleford to Lydney is a curious stone monument – with a large square base surmounted by a stone shaft – known as Gattle's Cross. Although probably not more than a couple of hundred years old, it is believed to have replaced an earlier stone that was erected in 1282. The earlier stone was known as 'Eleanor's Cross' and – according to tradition – marked the spot where Queen Eleanor rested on her journey from Wales. What became of this cross is not known.

Gattle's Cross, Sling.

It seems that Gattle's Cross may at some time have been the subject of a paranormal visitation. D.P. Sullivan, in his book *Old Stones of Gloucestershire*, reports receiving information that described how some years ago a local person saw the ghost of a man dressed in black near to the stone. The account is not very detailed, however, and although the sighting is likely to have taken place in the middle of the twentieth century, no further information was available.

SNOWSHILL

Various ghosts are said to have been heard or seen at the fascinating, and slightly odd-looking, Snowshill Manor. One room in the house is known as 'Ann's Room' and there is a local belief that it is haunted by the ghost of Ann Parsons, a young heiress who on St Valentine's Eve in 1604 was secretly married in an illegal ceremony at the house. Tradition has it that she had been brought there from Elmley Castle in Worcestershire by one Anthony Palmer, who was a servant in the household of a man named George Savage – to whom Ann was already betrothed. It seems likely that Ann had been secretly involved with Palmer, but it is unlikely that their romance lasted because the marriage was subsequently declared invalid.

The ghost of a man named Charles Marshall, a former occupant of Snowshill Manor, is supposed to have appeared on a black horse to one of his former employees, Richard Carter, on several occasions in the 1850s. Seeking assistance from the local rector, Carter was advised to say to the ghost 'What troublest thou, in the name of the Lord?'

When the ghost appeared again Carter followed the rector's advice, and the ghost asked him to be at the chaff house at the Manor at midnight. Carter kept the appointment and was again met by Marshall's ghost, who gave him a secret message to pass on to Mrs Marshall. It was never revealed what was in the secret message, but it was believed that the ghost had revealed where some hidden money might be found.

Years later, in 1919, Snowshill Manor was purchased by an eccentric character named Charles Wade, who used the place to house his enormous collection of antiques and curiosities. The place was at that time in a state of poor repair, and twenty-eight workmen engaged to undertake renovation stayed in the attic. After just one night one of the workmen refused to stay another night there, saying the place was haunted. Wade, who had inherited sugar estates in the West Indies from his father, was interested not only in artefacts, but also in astrology and alchemy, and it has been claimed by former servants at the house that he practised magic in a private room. This room is situated in an attic and is known as 'The Witch's Garret', housing an assortment of oddments connected with witchcraft. On one wall there is an illustration that includes two mandrakes, and an obscure circular design on the floor is believed to be of Rosicrucian origin. In 1951 Wade presented his house and collection of more than 22,000 items to The National Trust.

A servant at the house in the 1920s frequently heard footsteps in the corridor outside her room, yet when she opened the door there would be no sign of anyone – even though

Snowshill Manor, Snowshill.

the footsteps could still be heard. Apparently this was a very common occurrence and, although initially frightening, subsequently became accepted as a curious feature of the old house. In recent years, even, National Trust guides working at Snowshill Manor have heard unaccountable footsteps pacing across some of the rooms, and some visitors to the house have commented on an intense 'feeling' there. One of the rooms in the house is named 'Zenith', and it is said that a duel once took place there. One of the participants is supposed to have been killed, so it may be that this incident has added to the house's mysterious and ghostly atmosphere.

The village pub, The Snowshill Arms, is next door to Snowshill Manor. The place apparently has a ghost hound that causes visiting dogs to snarl at its presence, although no one has actually seen the ghostly canine. People seeing the reaction of their own canines have merely assumed the 'presence' to be that of an invisible ghost dog. In the 1970s a vague figure, said to resemble a hooded monk, was quite often seen in the upper part of the building. The figure would pass through walls or closed doors, and it is said that the pub's dog would react to its presence. During this period, too, there were various examples of minor poltergeist activity at the pub, with doors opening and closing by themselves.

There is said to be a strange 'presence' in the lane that runs past the pub and Snowshill Manor and there is a local belief that it is the unhappy ghost of a monk. Charles Wade, the eccentric and locally-popular owner of Snowshill Manor, spent much of his time in the

West Indies after giving Snowshill Manor to the National Trust in 1951 but within a few years was back in Snowshill forever. He came on a visit to England in 1956 but was taken ill in Broadway and soon after died in Evesham Hospital. He is buried with his mother and sisters in the churchyard at Snowshill. Beneath the sign of the cross on his tombstone are the words *IN HOC SIGNO SPES MEA*, which translates to 'In This Sign Is My Hope'. He is described on the memorial as:

ARTIST, COLLECTOR, ARCHITECT, CRAFTSMAN, POET.

SOUDLEY

Given the subject matter of this book, it is probably inevitable that bizarre tales of somewhat Fortean nature will occasionally come to light. An interesting and entertaining organisation named *Gloucestershire Paranormal and Fortean Investigations* has reported how in 2007 a curious letter was received by the Forest of Dean's weekly newspaper, *The Forester*. The correspondent described how, when walking around Soudley Pond in 2003, a strange animal was encountered. The creature was, apparently, a 'very fat round shaped animal that was brown and was flying without flapping its wings'.

Soudley Pond, Soudley.

It was subsequently suggested that the mystery animal might well be a mandarin duck that had strayed from the nearby Dean Heritage Centre. This would have seemed an entirely plausible explanation, were it not for the fact that *Gloucestershire Paranormal and Fortean Investigations* had in fact already received a report of the mystery animal of Soudley Pond, in which it was described as '4ft tall' and without a face. The strange creature was soon dubbed 'The Soudley Birdman', with *Gloucestershire Paranormal and Fortean Investigations* stating that 'details of any more sightings of the Soudley flying freak would be gratefully received'.

The story certainly has an aura of fantasy about it, but it may indeed be that some bizarre flying creature occasionally makes an appearance in the vicinity of Soudley Pond. In any case, it makes a refreshing change from the numerous reports of alien big cats in the Forest of Dean.

SOUTH CERNEY

South Cerney is fortunate to possess several pleasant drinking establishments, one of these being The Eliot Arms Hotel, beside the River Churn. For some years there have been stories of a resident ghost at the hotel, with a 'grey lady' having been seen in the building by several people. The ghost is not thought to be troublesome, although it must have been considered so at one time, because an exorcism was conducted there years ago. The ghost is still seen from time to time, though, so the exorcism seems to have been less than successful.

The ghost is most commonly seen in stormy weather, and a folklore tale seeks to account for its origin. Many years ago a mother and son were travelling in a horse and carriage outside the inn. A large tree fell onto the carriage – as the result of a storm – and killed both the occupants. They were brought into the inn, and although the son has never been seen, the troubled spirit of his mother still haunts the place.

Other peculiar tales are centred on the village. A report has been made that an unidentified flying object was seen in the dark sky above South Cerney in January 2009. A bright orange circular object, which seemed to have a small regularly-pulsing corona, was observed to move silently in a direct line across the sky. It was low flying and travelled at a constant speed, with the witness feeling sure that it was not a 'balloon' type object.

STANTON

Apparently at the intersection of two ley lines, Stanton is surely among the prettiest villages in the Cotswolds. The ancient Church of St Michael probably dates back to the ninth century, although much of the present building is of the fifteenth century. As with so many Cotswold churches, there are indications of ancient pagan origins, and there is an interesting 'green man' with a protruding tongue. Usually thought to be a pagan symbol of fertility and regeneration, the 'green man' is often seen with foliage sprouting from his mouth, but less commonly has his tongue actually sticking out.

The village's popular hostelry, The Mount Inn, is believed to be haunted by a ghost named 'Billy' – thought to be the inn's first landlord from the early years of the twentieth century. This ghost seems to be a poltergeist in nature, for its presence is usually indicated by moving glasses and opening doors. Once, however, a customer had a particularly unnerving experience when he saw a ghostly hand reach out from the solid stone of a nearby wall. Although the inn's Donnington ales are reasonably potent, the customer is said to have been completely sober at the time of the occurrence.

STANWAY

Dragons seem to feature in this part of Gloucestershire, and there are dragon-based tales from nearby Coombe Hill, Deerhurst and Tredington. A particularly fine representation of

St George slaying the dragon adorns the war memorial at Stanway, although this is intended as an illustration of the triumph of good over evil, rather than a local dragon-slaying legend.

In the Middle Ages this fictional monster was commonly used to represent evil, and it was during this period that the story of St George slaying the dragon circulated. Not much is known for certain about George's life, although it seems to be agreed among historians that he was born in the third century at Anatolia, a Greek-speaking town that is now part of modern-day Turkey. His parents were Christian and after becoming a Roman soldier George protested loudly about Rome's persecution of the Christians. As a result he was arrested and tortured, but stayed true to his beliefs. Executed by decapitation at Nicomedia in Palestine, he

St George slaying the Dragon, Stanway.

subsequently came to be closely associated with the triumph of good over evil, becoming patron Saint of England.

Marginally more common in the district than reports of fire-breathing dragons are apparent sightings of panther-like big cats. In the late 1980s a Police Sergeant stationed at Stow-on-the-Wold was driving up Stanway Hill at about 9 p.m. one evening, on his way to perform night duty, when he suddenly saw a 'big black animal' on the roadside. He recalls especially that the beast had 'two big orange eyes'. The officer, having worked through the night for many years, was very familiar with deer, badgers, foxes, dogs and the like, and although he could not positively identify the beast his thoughts turned to reports of big-cat sightings in the county and in neighbouring Worcestershire.

STAUNTON

Although surrounded by the dense forest and woodland that spreads virtually down to the banks of the River Wye in Wales, Staunton feels very much like the Gloucestershire Forest of Dean country. The village is particularly known for a number of peculiar and mysterious stones that surround it. One of these – a monolith of old red conglomerate, standing 6ft above the ground – is known as the Long Stone and is reputed to be the central point of a number of ley lines. It stands beside the road to Coleford and probably dates to the Bronze Age.

Probably the best-known stone in the village, however, is the Buckstone. Situated just above the village, on a hill from which there are extensive views across the River Wye and into Wales, the stone is a massive boulder of quartz conglomerate that undoubtedly weighs hundreds of tons. At one time there was a belief that the stone was used as a sacrificial altar by Druids, but there is no evidence to support this. It is a fact, however, that it was once a 'rocking stone', glacial movement having deposited it so that the stone could be moved on its pivotal axis with relative ease. The stone no longer rocks, though, having been dislodged by a party of travelling actors in 1885. The stone toppled onto the road below, breaking into several pieces, but was cemented together and set back on its pivot by the insertion of a steel reinforcing rod.

Staunton's other significant stone is a huge mass of quartz conglomerate rock in Highmeadow

The Long Stone, Staunton.

Above: *The Buckstone, Staunton.*

Above: *The Suckstone, Staunton.*

Right: *Near Hearkening Rock, Staunton.*

Woods. Called the Suckstone and often stated to be the 'largest boulder in England', the stone measures 60ft by 40ft and is clearly very big indeed. It is difficult to be sure of the weight of the Suckstone, and the figures of 4,000 and 14,000 tons are often quoted as realistic estimates – although figures as great as 30,000 and even 300,000 tons have been seen in print. Staff at the Tourist Information Office in Coleford have confirmed that the stone is in the parish of Staunton in Gloucestershire, although close scrutiny of an ordnance survey map has suggested that the Suckstone is technically just within Wales. Perhaps this is a case where both Gloucestershire and Monmouthshire can claim to have the 'largest boulder in Britain'. And whether actually Welsh or English, the stone looks to be very much a part of the Forest of Dean.

The impressive rocky buttresses of Near Hearkening Rock can be seen nearby, from where there are fine views over the Suckstone and into Wales. It is said that the rock acquired its name because small sounds are amplified by its concave face. It is probable that the Suckstone once formed a part of Near Hearkening Rock, becoming detached during glacial movement millions of years ago.

In addition to mysterious stones, the Staunton area apparently has some suspected big cats within its area. In 1994 a police inspector was driving near the village one morning when what was thought to be a panther leapt in front of his car. He described it as '…black, larger than a fox … about the size of a large dog.' A month later a Staunton couple driving from Newent one evening saw a cat-like creature that they claimed '… could not have been a domestic cat because its legs were too long. It was at least 2ft high. It wasn't a cat, it wasn't a fox and it was too high for a badger…' Then, a couple of weeks later, a black animal the size of a large dog was seen crossing the A417 road near the village. It remains to be seen whether similar reports are received in the twenty-first century.

STOW-ON-THE-WOLD

Like many towns and villages in the Cotswolds, Stow-on-the-Wold is reputed to have a virtual maze of subterranean tunnels and passages running beneath its roads and houses. Indeed, Harold Bagust, in his book *A History of Stow-on-the-Wold*, says that Stow has so many cellars and passages beneath it that it has been likened to a rabbit warren. However, he adds that most of them have now been sealed off. Local tradition has long held that a secret tunnel runs from The King's Arms Hotel in Stow Square to Maugersbury Manor. In 1976 a large vault beneath the road was revealed during excavation work in Stow Square, and a passageway led from it towards the north-east – approximately in the direction of The King's Arms Hotel. The vault and tunnel were not properly examined, however, and they were filled in before archaeologists could look at the discovery.

The King's Arms Hotel is around 500 years old and can boast that King Charles I stayed the night there on 8 May 1645. The place has for years been reputed to be haunted by a grey-haired old lady who wears a chain and pendant around her neck. The apparition of the lady has been seen on various occasions over many decades, most commonly seated in a large armchair in the lounge. A sighting of the ghost was reported to Andrew Green, author of the book *Ghosts of Today*, in 1962 then in 1986 or 1987 a lady staying at the hotel described how she saw an elderly woman, ascending the stairs ahead of her, suddenly vanish before reaching the top. Also, there have been numerous examples of minor poltergeist activity, such as doors opening and closing of their own accord and electric fires switching themselves on and off. These occurrences tend to be attributed to the antics of the resident ghost. No one knows the ghost's identity, though there has been a suggestion that she is a former owner of the hotel.

The Royalist Hotel in the town's Digbeth Street is even older than The King's Arms Hotel. Indeed, the *Guinness Book of Records* confirms it to be the oldest inn in England. The place was built in AD 947 and, perhaps unsurprisingly, is supposed to be very haunted. The apparition of an elderly lady is said to have been seen in an upper floor corridor on at least two occasions in the 1970s, and in the 1980s it was reported that one room was supposedly the regular scene of paranormal activity. In general, however, reports and descriptions are vague – although a clairvoyant visiting the hotel has apparently sensed an array of ghostly entities in the building. These included young children, dogs, a lady in a long lace dress, a Cavalier and even a knight in armour. The clairvoyant also claimed that a man had died in the area between the bar and the reception desk. The perceptive senses of most visitors to the hotel seem to be rather less keen, however, and no other reports of this curious spectral host have yet been received.

Stow-on-the-Wold's hotels are, if reports are to be believed, very popular with visitors from beyond the grave. Stow Lodge Hotel, just off the market square, is another of the town's hospitality establishments that has a ghost story connected to it. One room in particular, has been the focus of paranormal activity. A guest staying some years ago awoke one night to see a hideous (though otherwise rather indistinct) presence at the foot of his bed. In a state of terror, the guest tore the wooden leg off a nearby sideboard and began to thrash wildly at the ghostly visitation. There appears to be no record of the outcome, but it is assumed that the unwelcome entity was persuaded to make a hasty exit. More recently guests staying in the room heard and sensed some kind of strange presence there, although on this occasion it left after a matter of seconds, perhaps fearing a sound beating with an improvised wooden club.

As recently as the twenty-first century yet more peculiar activity occurred, however, another room was the scene on this occasion. A man was seated alone on the bed in his room while his wife went out to visit some shops and, as he watched television, felt someone sit down beside him. Yet, as he turned to greet what he assumed must be his returning wife, there was no one there. On the bedding, however, was the distinct impression left by 'whoever' had sat down. One assumes the husband smoothed it flat again before his wife's return.

Customers at The White Hart Hotel were startled by a sudden episode of poltergeist activity in the bar late one evening in the mid-1990s. Quite without warning, all of the pictures hanging on the wall abruptly turned so that they hung at a peculiar ninety degree angle, almost as though the building had been shaken by an earthquake. No tremor had

Stow Lodge Hotel, Stow-on-the-Wold.

taken place, though, and the licensee calmly explained that the incident was probably the work of a poltergeist that was believed responsible for regularly placing a hunting horn – that usually hung on the wall – down upon the floor, where it was often found early in the morning.

Ghostly activity that has been reported at The Old Stocks Hotel seems rather more benign and welcome. The pleasant sound of piano music has been heard by diners in the hotel restaurant and by residents staying in a particular room, which is rather strange since no piano was in fact actually being played in either room at the time. A former owner of the hotel, the Reverend Alan Burr, was known to play the piano and although he died many years ago there is a suspicion that it is his ghost that plays the ethereal, and so far unidentified, music. An apparition of the cleric is said to have been seen, too, and in 1989 a guest staying in the same room reported that she awoke in the middle of the night to find an elderly male figure in vicar's robes leaning over her prone body. The figure had a chain around his neck, wore half-moon spectacles and was moving his hands along the outline of her body as she lay in bed. The spectral figure vanished within seconds, though, its sudden appearance and rather dubious behaviour being reported to staff the following morning.

The final case involving mysterious activity at Stow-on-the-Wold involves a fairly short-lived poltergeist haunting. The focus seems to have been a fourteen-year-old boy with the surname of Pethrick, who lived with his family at a house in Chapel Street, off

Stow's Well Lane. This poltergeist was from 1963 to 1964 quite vigorous and disruptive, and publicity followed – with the case going on to feature in a number of books on ghosts and haunted houses. Accounts of the apparently bizarre and inexplicable activities have been oft-repeated, although there rarely seems to have been any really objective examination or analysis.

Problems began when pools of water started inexplicably appearing about the house and, when officials attended, no cause could be found. Furniture began to move of its own volition, the son was apparently 'tipped out of bed', sheets were ripped and clothing is said to have thrust itself under a mattress. The headboard of the boy's bed was unaccountably gouged and scarred, and writing appeared on some of the walls in the house. Alarmingly, a baby's hand appeared from the end of the boy's bed, slowly changed into that of a child, and then became a man's fully-grown hand. Who saw this happen? Were there any independent witnesses? Finally a voice was heard – from where and by whom? – saying that one of the builders of the house, who had died twenty years earlier, was causing the problems. It is claimed that enquiries revealed that the poltergeist activity had begun on the anniversary of the man's death.

The Pethrick family went on holiday to Devon, and the poltergeist apparently went with them. This does seem to suggest that the poltergeist activity was being 'caused' by the boy – though not necessarily consciously – rather than centred on the house in Chapel Street. The family became friendly with the local vicar and it is said that with his help the poltergeist 'transferred itself to the church'. It seems likely that some form of exorcism service took place, with the desired positive outcome. This case has a number of features common to many poltergeist incidences of haunting, being of short duration and focused on a pubescent child.

STROUD

It is surprising that relatively few legends and ghost stories have come to light from the town of Stroud, although it will have been seen that elsewhere in this book tales from several of its surrounding villages have been described. Almost inevitably, at least a couple of Stroud's pubs are said to have a resident ghost. The town's premier live music venue, The Golden Fleece Inn, apparently has a ghost named 'Jack', who moves glasses around and causes staff and customers to sometimes feel that a presence is behind them even when no one else is in the vicinity. The Greyhound pub, in the town centre, proudly owns a fine set of Grade II listed gentlemen's lavatories. Whether the pub's resident ghost, 'George', feels at home using these Victorian facilities is not known, but his presence is made known by minor poltergeist activities such as the switching on and off of electric lights, the lighting of candles, and the smashing of glasses. Such occurrences might seem somewhat humdrum were it not for the fact that they have often happened when no human hand was anywhere near.

The apparition of a cyclist careering out of control and over a hedge on Stroud Hill Road has allegedly been seen a couple of times in the years that followed soon after the

First World War. It seemed so real to those who saw it that searches were carried out to try and locate the rider and bicycle, but nothing was ever found. It seems possible that many years ago a tragic bicycle accident took place on the hill, and that for some time after a kind of visual 'replay' was seen by persons sensitive to such things.

Claims of a rather more earthly mystery came to light when in January 2008 it was claimed by a big cat expert that animal tracks found in the snow near Stroud were left by a predatory big cat. Four days later a roe deer was found dead less than a mile away, having been 'extensively eaten by a large predator'. The big cat expert, Frank Tunbridge, stated his belief that a big cat was responsible for the death of the deer. A little over a year later, in the spring of 2009, CCTV cameras at a Stroud industrial estate filmed what Tunbridge described as a 'jungle cat hybrid' at least 3ft in length.

TETBURY

This town has been the focus of several cases of mysterious activity, and even its annual Woolsack Races that take place each May Day Bank Holiday Monday are an interesting folk tradition with seventeenth-century origins. Connected with the town's wool trade, the races involve teams of four who run in relays, carrying a 60lb woolsack up and down

Chavenge House, Tetbury.

Gumstool Hill. The hill's name is taken from a 'gumstool' – apparently a device similar to a ducking stool that was used to duck unfortunate women in a pond at the foot of the hill.

A splendid Elizabethan manor house named Chavenage House, said to have been the scene of paranormal activity, can be seen just over a mile to the north-west of Tetbury. During the Civil War the house was owned by Colonel Nathaniel Stephens, a Parliamentarian and MP for Gloucestershire, whom Oliver Cromwell tried to persuade to agree to the execution of Charles I. The colonel gave his agreement, and the king was beheaded in 1649, but the colonel's daughter, Abigail, was enraged by this, apparently, laying a curse upon her father for bringing the family name into disrepute. In due course Colonel Stephens died and it is said that as relatives assembled in the courtyard of Chavenage House in readiness for the funeral, a coach drawn by black horses pulled up and the shrouded figure of the colonel was seen to glide into the coach. As the coach departed it vanished in a burst of flames.

This ghostly spectacle is not the only apparition said to have been seen at Chavenage House. The headless ghost of King Charles I was seen there soon after his execution, and the house is supposed to be haunted by the ghost of Abigail, the colonel's daughter. Not every haunting in the area has such illustrious connections, however. The Royal Oak inn at Cirencester Road dates from 1630, and has long been reputed as the dwelling place of a mischievous poltergeist, with several reports of glasses being seen to fly off shelves..

Mysteries continue into the twenty-first century, and as recently as the summer of 2008 a UFO sighting report was received from the town. A total of nine orange lights were seen moving silently above Tetbury for around three or four minutes. The spherical objects moved steadily as if in formation, and the witness – an ex-RAF Air Traffic Controller and qualified Meteorological Observer – felt certain that the lights were not those of conventional aircraft. The incident was reported to the Police, the RAF subsequently confirming that they were unaware of any activity in the area.

TEWKESBURY

A green field known as Bloody Meadow, not far from Tewkesbury Abbey, was once the scene of appalling butchery and slaughter and no doubt still retains an air of unhappiness and hostility for some sensitive people.

For years the Houses of York and Lancaster had been struggling for the succession to the English throne when, on 4 May 1471, King Edward IV of the House of York closed with the Lancastrian forces commanded by the Duke of Somerset. This confrontation with the army of Queen Margaret of Anjou took place at what at that time was called Gaston Field. King Edward's men gained the upper hand and the Lancastrians fled, hotly pursued through the streets of Tewkesbury. The fleeing men were caught in a meadow beside the river and slaughtered.

The Duke of Somerset and some of his lords had taken sanctuary in Tewkesbury Abbey but were shown no mercy however, and were dragged out, summarily tried, then publicly

Bloody Meadow, Tewkesbury.

executed. Somerset was beheaded in the town's market square. Among those dragged out of the abbey and killed was Edward, Prince of Wales. The apparition of a young man wearing a velvet jacket, said to have occasionally been seen near the abbey, is thought to be that of the young prince. Given the dreadful slaughter that took place, it is little wonder that the abbey and its surroundings are said to be haunted. A white lady is said to appear at the Abbey Foregate and glide along the path into the churchyard. Usually she vanishes, but has been witnessed to turn and face the Foregate, before giving a piercing scream of terror. Ghostly moans and screams have been heard in the abbey, and a black monk has been seen in an aisle, before surmounting an invisible staircase and vanishing from view.

Tewkesbury Abbey itself has some grim reminders of that awful episode, in the form of jagged strips of metal that have been used to plate the vestry door. These are the remnants of pieces of armour collected from the battlefield, displayed to illustrate the violation of sanctuary sought by survivors of the battle. The abbey has other curious signs and representations of mysterious origin. Several piers in the nave have had a pentagram – the sign of the witches – scratched into the stone. This is probably some form of ancient graffiti. Additionally, there are various 'green men' throughout the abbey. These pagan symbols – believed to represent fertility and regeneration – can be seen in the nave, side chapels, south aisle and elsewhere in the building.

A number of the town's inns and pubs are reputed to be haunted. Ye Olde Black Bear, believed to be the oldest of these, has the ghost of a tall man who wears a tarnished breastplate

Tewkesbury Abbey.

and is sometimes seen standing at a window looking out at the River Severn that flows past the end of the garden. It has been claimed that the apparition is that of a Yorkist soldier who was wounded in battle and brought to the house, where he died a few days later.

In 1994 *The Gloucestershire Echo* newspaper reported that The Bell Hotel in Tewkesbury's Church Street had been visited by a ghost-hunter who claimed that the ghosts of soldiers killed in the battle haunted the top bedroom, which still retained its original fourteenth-century timber frames. Apparently, the ghosts were the restless spirits of men who had not received a Christian burial.

Other ghosts haunting the town's licensed premises seem unconnected with the town's bloody battle. Tapping noises and unexplained footsteps have for years been heard at The Berkeley Arms and apparently the place has a ghost who throws open the front door, and then loudly ascends the stairs before disappearing. When an internal wall was demolished in the 1970s a secret room was revealed, and it is claimed that ghostly footsteps have been heard heading in that direction.

The Tudor House Hotel is said to have a ghostly white lady who haunts the upper floors of the building. Also seen in and around the building is the curious apparition of a phantom black dog although, unlike the devilish 'hell hounds' sometimes reported from other parts of the county, this spectral animal seems placid.

Although most of Tewkesbury's mysterious occurrences are connected with the battle of 1471, there have been some reports of strange activities in the skies above the town. Several claimed UFO sightings seem to have perfectly straightforward explanations involving the presence of Chinese lanterns or even a police helicopter, but one report from an off-duty police officer in 1976 is less easy to explain away. The officer's description of the event brings to mind scenes from low-budget science fiction movies, but readers must make up their own minds.

The time was 12.30 a.m. and the officer had just returned to his home, which backed onto the M5 motorway at Tewkesbury. He had recently concluded a late evening duty shift at Cheltenham Police Station, although it is not known how busy he had been or whether he had rounded off his tour of duty with a pint or two of ale at the Police Club – as was a common practice in the 1970s. Whatever the case, the officer saw a 'huge cross-shaped UFO' in the skies behind his home. The UFO, he claimed, was similar in size to a civil airliner and he watched it slowly rotate at a height of about 50ft above the quiet motorway. Ominously, the strange craft began moving across the fields towards his home, and he saw that there was a red light at the centre of the cross formed by its arms. The officer ran into his house – not to escape the UFO's attentions as one might imagine, but to get a torch, which he flashed at the object. Perhaps in fear of the torch's beam, the UFO reacted by slowly backing away over the motorway. It then performed an interesting manoeuvre that involved the spinning of the craft's body on the axis of one of its arms, before moving off and out of sight.

Although this report seems fantastic – some might say ludicrous – it may have been noticed that there seems to have been a small flurry of UFO-related activity in this part of the county during the mid-1970s. There may be a temptation to dismiss this story as fantasy or invention, but what could one stand to gain from making such a report? It is easy to see, however, that such an account could very easily become part of local folklore.

THRUPP

Nether Lypiatt Manor, to the south-east of Stroud, has for years been considered haunted. Indeed, when in 1981 the house was bought by Prince and Princess Michael of Kent, it was apparently obtained at a reasonable price because other potential purchasers were discouraged by rumours of the house being haunted.

The house was built between 1702 and 1705 by notorious hanging judge Charles Coxe, who was renowned for administering harsh justice. According to legend, a blacksmith was put before the judge for the crime of sheep-stealing. The blacksmith already had convictions for offences of theft, so hanging was to be the likely sentence. The judge saw a use for the hapless blacksmith, however. Nether Lypiatt Manor needed a pair of wrought iron gates at the entrance, and Judge Coxe decided that if the blacksmith created a suitably impressive pair by the time the next legal circuit had been completed he would be reprieved.

With every incentive to produce the goods, the blacksmith set to work, and on his return in 1705 Judge Coxe found the impressive pair of gates that can still be seen today.

Nether Lypiatt Manor, Thrupp.

An ornate metal plate on the gates bore the double-interlocking initials 'C'. Judge Charles Coxe was a merciless man, however, and after spotting a tiny flaw on one of the gates he sent the blacksmith to the gallows.

The unfortunate man was hanged on 25 January 1705, but – so the story goes – on that night a fierce gust of wind blew the gates open. There, beside the ornate metal plate, sat the phantom of the hanged blacksmith, mounted on a white stallion. He shook his fist angrily at the judge, who was watching from a window, before vanishing. It is said that Coxe died from a mystery illness a few weeks later – although he actually died in 1728. Some claim that, even to the present day, the spectre of the blacksmith appears by the iron gates. Judge Coxe's son, too, came to no good and it is said that he hanged himself in one of the rooms at the house. His ghost is said to appear around the place from time to time. It has to be said, though, that in more than twenty-five years of residence at the house Prince and Princess Michael experienced nothing ghostly at all there.

TIRLEY

When taking the B4213 road from Cheltenham and Tewkesbury towards the M50 motorway, one passes over the River Severn at Haw Bridge about half a mile south-east of Tirley village. The scene today is relatively quiet, with the welcoming Haw Bridge

Inn standing beside the river. The bridge, which affords uninterrupted views of the river from a footway running beside its parapet, was opened in 1961 when its predecessor was badly damaged by a runaway barge in 1958.

The scene was not always so tranquil. Twenty years earlier, in January 1938, the bridge and river beneath hit the headlines when a gruesome discovery was made by fishermen netting the water.

The River Severn at Haw Bridge, Tirley.

A man's headless and limbless torso – subsequently believed to be that of one Captain William Butt – was caught in the net, precipitating a major police investigation. This was obviously a case of murder, which was suspected to have been committed by one Brian Sullivan – who had earlier been found dead at Cheltenham, having apparently committed suicide. Although a connection was established between Butt and Sullivan, a substantial search of Sullivan's home and garden failed to reveal anything definitive. And although the human remains were almost certainly Butt's, this could not be proven since the head never did turn up. The mystery remains, then, as an unsolved 'murder of a person or persons unknown' – with the River Severn at Haw Bridge perhaps concealing the remains of Captain William Butt's skull. (*see* also under entry for Cheltenham.)

TODENHam

This village's inn, The Farriers Arms, may date in part from the seventeenth century. A former landlady has described how in the 1970s and '80s she often saw two small white dogs running silently up the stairs that lead from the lounge bar to the private quarters of the inn. These 'ghost dogs' – which would fade into the walls about halfway up the stairway – were seen by several guests, too, who were staying at the inn. Also, the apparitional hooded figure of a monk was seen by both the landlady and her son, independently of each other, in one of the bedrooms during the late 1970s, although there is no clue as to the origin of this spectral figure.

It seems, too, that alien wild cats may reside in the Todenham area. In 2009 a woman living on the edge of the village reported seeing what resembled a lynx or hyena, with distinctive tufted ears and mottled brown coat, in a gateway a few yards away. The peculiar animal was visible for several minutes, before it moved away.

TREDINGTON

Legends of dragons and sea serpents are not uncommon in this part of Gloucestershire, with the nearby villages of Deerhurst and Coombe Hill having at one time suffered the attentions of these monsters. Accounts are of course based on legend and folklore. At the small village of Tredington, however, there is an unusual remnant of a creature from long ago, and it may be that this was known of by the residents of the nearby villages.

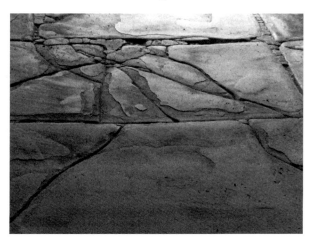

Fossil of Ichthyosaurus, Tredington.

The village of Tredington has a Norman church, part of which dates from the twelfth century. Embedded in the flagstones that pave the south porch is a fossilized ichthyosaurus – a prehistoric fish-like reptile that dates from the early Jurassic age. These creatures, which are an ancestor of modern-day dolphins, started to evolve around 200 million years ago. The ichthyosaurus was usually around 6ft long, so the Tredington example, which measures 9ft in length, is a particularly large specimen.

Arthur Mee, editor of the book *The King's England: Gloucestershire*, describes how coming into the church involves 'walking over a monster which had its day and ceased to be before the first man walked the earth'.

It is easy to imagine how this fossilized 'fish-lizard' lying at the entrance to the village church must have seemed frightening to our ancestors. And it is not difficult to envisage how, hundreds of years ago, it might have been regarded as the remains of a slain serpent. So, then, is Tredington's fossilized ichthyosaurus perhaps the source of local sea-serpent legends?

UPTON ST LEONARDS

Roy Palmer, in his book *Folklore of Gloucestershire*, describes a story that illustrates how a murderer's victim was brought to justice by the intervention of the dead man's ghost. The tale is thin on detail, and seems an unlikely yarn, but is no doubt based on a centuries-old folklore belief that originated as a warning to potential wrong-doers.

The story goes that a carpenter in the village was one day found lying dead in his garden. The cause of death seems not to have been established, but he had previously been of good health, and it began to be rumoured that his wife had murdered him. There was no evidence to support this suspicion, however, and no one was able to say how she might have done the deed. Following the death, a large, dark, shapeless spectre began to haunt the churchyard, even appearing to the parson.

Whether the ghost continued to haunt the churchyard is not known, but some twenty years later the dead carpenter appeared in a dream to the parson, advising him that something would happen next day to solve the mystery of his sudden death. Following this, the parson approached the sexton, who was digging a grave, and told him what the ghost had said. As the sexton dug the new grave, he suddenly began turning up bones from an earlier burial, including a skull. Displaying remarkable skills in the science of pathology, the sexton recognized the skull as being that of the dead carpenter. This was no ordinary sexton – he went on to carefully examine the skull, finding that a brass pin had been driven deeply into the back of it.

This new evidence was put to the carpenter's widow, apparently, and she confessed to murdering him. She would probably have been hanged, but she became ill and died soon after the confession.

Something large and black was seen in Upton St. Leonards in 1994, though it was not in the churchyard, nor was it any kind of ghost. A man walking his dog through woodland near the M5 embankment saw an animal about 150 yards from where he was standing. Watching it closely with the aid of a telescope, he later said, 'I was certain that it was a big cat … it was black with slightly grey hind legs, which looked very powerful. It seemed to be injured and was moving very sluggishly.'

WESTBURY-ON-SEVERN

In her book *True Ghost Stories of the Forest of Dean*, Dena Bryant-Duncan describes how, when she moved in 1998 to live at The Manse in Westbury, she realised the place retained some 'residents'. The sound of scampering footsteps running up and down the stairs was heard, and a door to a cupboard beneath the stairs unlatched itself and opened. The apparition of a young gentleman 'not from our time' was seen in an ancient pantry room, and on one memorable occasion two Royalist officers came running down the stairs, then turned and saluted before leaving through the front door! Additionally, The Manse has a hooded figure and a pipe-smoking ghost. It appears that either the building is exceptionally haunted or that Dena Bryant-Duncan has unusual powers of perception.

The Red Lion Inn, a Tudor building that stands close to the A48 road through Westbury, was apparently used as a hospital for soldiers wounded in a battle between Roundheads and Cavaliers in 1644. The Royalists had garrisoned the church, but were overcome by the Parliamentarian force commanded by Colonel Edward Massey. The inn has over the years been the focus of several paranormal activities. Things have been 'moved about' in the cellar, and cutlery placed neatly at tables at night has by the next morning been found scattered around the place.

One curious tale involves a regular customer named 'Harry'. He used to regularly complain about the church and said that he would never set foot in the place, and that when he died he certainly didn't want to be buried in the churchyard. One day Harry died suddenly and, in keeping with his wishes, he was not taken into the building for the funeral service. While the service took place, the undertaker – with Harry in his coffin – waited at the church gates. The reception was to take place at The Red Lion Inn, so the landlord and his wife were last to arrive at the service, having securely locked the inn doors.

As soon as the service was over they made their way back to the inn, only to find the doors not only open, but securely fastened back. Yet there was no one in the inn. The undertaker confirmed that he had seen no one approach the building, and Harry was quite definitely still in his coffin! But it was felt that he had had the last laugh. Perhaps, in spirit form, he had opened up the doors to his old haunt to ensure he would be the first to get a drink.

WINCHCOMBE

This small and attractive town was once a place of great importance. In Saxon times it was the capital of Winchcombshire in the Kingdom of Mercia, and a great abbey was founded in the town by King Kenulf around AD 798. Kenulf died soon after, leaving a seven-year-old son, Kenelm, and two daughters. It is around Kenelm that a legend has long been told, recorded in the eleventh century by Florence of Winchester and Geoffrey of Monmouth, although it was probably widely spoken of long before then.

Quendreda, the elder of King Kenulf's daughters, intended to become Queen of Mercia following her father's death. In order to succeed in this aim, she first needed to dispose of her young brother, so she persuaded her lover, Ascobert, to murder Kenelm. Ascobert took the boy hunting in the Clent Hills and, when the boy fell asleep after the hunt, began digging his grave. It is at this point that the story takes on a colourful air that one may feel has more to do with the telling of a good story than with fact. Kenelm suddenly awoke and announced the words, 'This is not the place ordained for you to kill me.' He planted an ash twig into the ground, and it blossomed with black buds and dark flowers – this apparently being seen as a token that what the boy had said was true.

Nevertheless, Ascobert did go on to kill Kenelm. He chopped off his head on the way home, burying both body and head under a thorn-bush. Before the grave was filled in, however, a white dove flew from the base of the boy's skull. It flew to Rome, where the diligent bird dropped a scroll at the Pope's feet. Kenelm's murder by his sister was revealed in the document, and the Pope sent orders to England that the body be searched for. The legend asserts that a white cow frequented the area in which Kenelm was buried, and this useful beast guided the searchers – monks from Winchcombe Abbey – to the grave. As they rested beside the body on the slopes of Sudeley Hill a holy spring suddenly gushed forth from the ground. The well, within a little well-house originating from the sixteenth century, can still be seen about a mile east of Sudeley Castle.

Kenelm's body was taken to Winchcombe Abbey and laid beside that of his father, King Kenulf. The boy's wicked sister watched the funeral procession pass and cursed it by reading Psalm 108 backwards. She got her just deserts, however, and her eyes burst out of her head as the hearse passed. It is now accepted that the legend of Kenelm is entirely fiction, but the yarn did no harm to the prosperity of Winchcombe Abbey. The shrine of St Kenelm was much visited and many miracles were said to have occurred there.

In the sixteenth century Leland stated that Kenelm was buried beside his father in the east end of the church. Following the Reformation, the abbey church fell into ruin, with two stone coffins being found at the east end of the foundations during excavations in 1815. The coffins contained the bones of a grown man and a child – a long knife lying beside the child, which was considered to be the body of Kenelm. The two coffins are displayed in Winchcombe church, although the bones and knife are said to have disintegrated when exposed to the air.

There is much folklore concerning the monks of Winchcombe Abbey. In Abbey Terrace a hostelry known as The Plaisterer's Arms has a subterranean passage called the 'monks' retreat'. Once a cellar, the room has a wall painted with the ominous-looking figure of a hooded monk. There is a tradition that the wall conceals a tunnel that once led to Winchcombe Abbey.

Ghostly monks have reportedly been seen in various parts of the town. A hooded figure has been seen in a lane called 'The Monk's Walk', with just the upper part of the body visible, suggesting that the level of the road has been raised. The figure faded then disappeared as it was being observed. The eerie sounds of religious chanting and choirs

Stone coffin at Winchcombe Church.

singing have been heard on the old abbey site, usually at midnight, and a monk-like figure has been seen walking along the road from Winchcombe to Greet.

Winchcombe also has a white lady ghost. It seems that every other town or village in the Cotswolds has some kind of misty, white phantom – although, more often than not, it proves difficult to find someone who has seen the ghost within recent years. One local man has, however, described how in the 1970s he was riding his motorcycle along the High Street at around 2 a.m. one morning when, as he drew level with the church, he saw a white female figure glide across the road just in front of him. There has long been a superstition locally of a white female spectre that glides from a cottage opposite the

Devil figure at Winchcombe Church.

church and into the churchyard, and this witness claims he definitely saw it.

Being only 9 miles from Tredington, from where there are tales of serpents and dragons, it is noticeable that Winchcombe, too, seems conscious of the dragon threat. Half of the forty gargoyles that adorn the church depict dragons or dragon-like creatures, while others depict demons and caricatures of local dignitaries. A hideous figure above the east window is thought to show the Devil himself and a startlingly evil-looking demon stares down from above the south porch.

The most famous resident of Sudeley Castle was Queen Katherine Parr, widow of King Henry VIII. She lived there with her fourth husband, Thomas Seymour, uncle to King Edward VI, but died in childbirth. Prince Rupert, nephew of King Charles I established his headquarters at Sudeley Castle during the Civil War, and the building was subsequently more or less destroyed by Cromwell's troops. The castle lay in ruins for many years, but in the nineteenth century was purchased and restored to its former glory.

There are reported to be two ghosts that haunt the castle. One is said to be that of Prince Rupert's favourite hunting dog, killed in the first siege of the castle. The phantom dog is most commonly seen in the ruins of the banqueting hall, its sighting said to be a harbinger of misfortune. The second ghost is that of a former housekeeper. Described by Andrew Green, in his book *Ghosts of Today*, the apparition has been seen by various visitors to come out of the Rupert Room and also in the main bedroom. Apparently, she wears a long pink-and-white skirt, a white blouse, a mob cap and black shoes.

Katherine Parr's body is interred in the castle's chapel, and, as far as is known, no one has seen her in ghostly form. In the eighteenth century – more than two centuries after her death – her body was subjected to depraved and sinister interference, however, so it is perhaps a wonder that she has not returned to haunt the scene. In 1782 a farmer named John Lucas found her coffin – one assumes among the ruins of the castle and its chapel – and opened it, to find the perfectly preserved body of the queen therein. It was said that the skin was white and moist. Lucas re-sealed the coffin, apparently, but it seems that he and his friends would not leave the queen in peace. The coffin was opened on a number of further occasions and the body was interfered with by Lucas and his drunken friends. The *Transactions of the Bristol and Gloucestershire Archaeological Society* record that they 'treated the remains in a gruesome and disgusting manner'. The coffin and the queen's body have, thankfully, been allowed to rest in peace since that disgraceful episode.

Far older than Winchcombe Abbey, Sudeley Castle, or any of the buildings in the town, is Belas Knap long barrow, which is approached by a steeply-wooded track, reached from Corndean Lane just outside Winchcombe. This Neolithic, chambered, long barrow dates from about 3800 BC, and when excavated in the 1860s was found to contain the skeletons of thirty-one people. The tomb is a place of great atmosphere and solitude, so it is perhaps unsurprising that some people have reported experiencing strange sensations there.

In the later years of the twentieth century a woman visiting the long barrow noticed a procession of monks walking across the field to where she was standing close to the mound. She backed off for a short while to afford the monks some privacy, but they failed to arrive and, when she returned to where she had been standing, she found that they had disappeared and the scene had changed, with fewer trees and a different field pattern. It may be that, momentarily, she saw an earlier scene through a 'window in time'.

Another report of a strange experience has been recorded – this time involving a family who decided to set up a substantial picnic on top of the long barrow. Apparently, it was a warm and calm day, and the family set out a tablecloth, cutlery, crockery and the like. Given the serene weather conditions, they were shocked when the cloth and its contents flew up into the air – scattering the items all around. Mysterious activity, indeed, although perhaps equally strange is why anyone would want to take a picnic on top of a grave.

Some people are undoubtedly more sensitive and perceptive than others. On one occasion a man and woman visiting the long barrow saw greenish 'orbs' in the vicinity and felt a 'presence' in the nearby woods. The couple sat side by side in the main burial chamber of the barrow, then became aware of a strange 'pins-and-needles' sensation – so powerful that they felt their limbs vibrating. They then heard slow, rhythmic drum sounds that seemed to come from outside the chamber. The sounds stopped as suddenly as they had begun and, feeling distinctly uneasy, the couple left the barrow and retuned to the road below the hill.

An excellent preserved steam railway, the Gloucestershire-Warwickshire Railway, runs from Toddington to Winchcombe, and on to Cheltenham. Travelling to Winchcombe railway station involves passing through a tunnel 693 yards long – the second longest tunnel on a preserved steam line. A Winchcombe man, now employed as a train driver on the national rail network, has described how as a youth of sixteen he saw an apparition at the mouth of the tunnel.

The year was 1977 and the railway had been closed for about a year. The youth was with friends larking about near the old tunnel, when he saw the figure of what he took to be a railwayman about twenty yards away, walking towards them. He looked away briefly, intending to tell his friends to run for it, but something made him look back again. The figure had vanished, yet there was nowhere it could have gone so quickly. The 'railwayman' had been wearing a cap and working clothes, but on reflection the youth recalled that the clothes had been somewhat old-fashioned and the figure's face was pale and white. Although walking on rough stone ballast, the figure had made no sound.

None of the other youths had seen the figure, but the man was quite certain of what he had seen – so certain, in fact, that he recorded the incident in his diary when he got home. He was later to hear that a railway worker had been killed near the tunnel in the 1920s and wondered if he had seen an apparition of the unfortunate victim.

Winchcombe's former police station is a stone building situated in Greet Road at its junction with North Street. It ceased to be a police station some years ago, but one officer stationed there during the late 1970s and early 1980s experienced numerous sightings of the apparition of a young boy. The figure was always seen in the same place – at the top of

The former police station in Winchcombe.

the stairs leading to the first floor, where there had at one time been living accommodation. The policeman always saw the figure out of the corner of his eye and, when he turned to see it more clearly, the image vanished. Once, the officer ran up the stairs to where the figure had been, and although there was nothing unusual to be seen he felt a 'block' of ice-cold air. The officer was far from superstitious or nervous, but he found the atmosphere there very unpleasant.

The policeman, intrigued by the apparition, made enquiries to try and ascertain its origin. He discovered that many years earlier a young boy had lived with his family at the first-floor accommodation, but had sadly died in the police station building. It was never ascertained for certain whether the apparition was of that young boy, but it does seem quite feasible. In any case, the appearances were of relatively short duration, and the 'ghost boy' was not seen after the early 1980s.

Finally, a couple of Winchcombe's pubs are considered haunted. The best known of the pub-dwelling ghosts is at The Old Corner Cupboard Inn, where the patter of tiny feet has often been heard running across a floor, and straight through a wall. The ghost, which is heard but never seen, is believed to be that of a little girl. At the other end of the town, The Old White Lion Inn in North Street is said to be haunted by a teenager named 'Elisabeth', who hanged herself in one of the rooms. The ghost seems harmless enough, apparently confining her activity to the unlocking of an attic door near the room.

WITHINGTON

Situated in a lovely setting close to the River Coln, The Mill Inn is a popular village hostelry and attracts many visitors throughout the year. It cannot be known how many of those visitors are aware of the ghosts that are said to reside at the inn, but for many years the place has been reputed to be haunted, with features appearing in the local press and mention of the ghosts being made in various books.

A *Gloucestershire Echo* feature in 1990 described how the licensee had seen various apparitions there. In particular, an old woman was on a number of occasions seen sitting in a fireside chair. She wore a wide-brimmed hat with a veil over her face, and standing behind her were the somewhat indistinct outlines of two men. Who the old woman and her shadowy gentleman companions were can only be guessed at, but the style of her clothing suggested she was from an earlier century. There is a traditional local belief that a former landlady drowned many years ago in the river that flows past the inn, and her ghost is supposed to haunt the building – although there is no report of any recent sighting.

WOODCHESTER

The great unfinished Woodchester Mansion in the valley of Woodchester Park must surely rank among the most eerie buildings in Gloucestershire. The estate was bought by William

The unfinished mansion at Woodchester Park.

Leigh in 1845, and he engaged a local architect, Benjamin Bucknall, to design a substantial neo-Gothic mansion. Building work began in 1854 and within four or five years was well advanced, then in 1870 work suddenly stopped. Builders downed tools and walked out, even leaving scaffolding in position and ladders propped up against walls. Most of the structural work had already been done, but the house was far from finished. Rooms were open to the roof, doors lead nowhere and upper corridors ended abruptly, with the ground visible far below.

So, what was the reason for the sudden abandonment of what had been a major ambition? It remains something of a mystery, though it is quite probable that Leigh had over-reached himself financially. He died a few years later and the mansion remained in an unfinished condition, inevitably deteriorating with the passage of time. It was bought by Stroud District Council in the mid-1980s and a trust was set up for the preservation of the house.

The strangely lifeless mansion, with its carvings and gargoyles depicting mythical creatures and pagan images, is said to be host to various paranormal phenomena, and there are numerous ghost stories connected to the house and the estate in which it is situated. Within the thousand-acre Woodchester Park there are five lakes, and these, too, feature in some of the stories of ghostly activity. A headless horseman is supposed to ride around one of the lakes, the explanation for this ghost's appearance being a convoluted account of how a villainous Sir Rupert de Lansigny committed murder in order to try and obtain the estate. He, in turn, was killed by a friend of the murder victim's family. The lakes are the backdrop for another ghostly image – that of a coffin that floats on the surface of one of them. The traditional explanation for this is that the coffin, which held the body of a suicide victim from King's Stanley, was set adrift on the water.

The park is haunted by several more interesting figures – those of a Roman centurion, a scruffy dwarf, and a Dominican monk who died by drowning after the ice on the lake he was skating on proved too thin to bear his weight. A horse and rider, believed to be of the seventeenth century, have been seen (and heard) clip-clopping along the drive, and a phantom coach with four horses has been seen passing through the mansion gates. American GI soldiers were billeted near the park during the Second World War, which may account for the reported sighting of two ghostly GIs smoking as they strolled through the parkland. Some of the American troops were involved in military exercises at the park in 1944, and it is said that a collapsing pontoon caused more than twenty deaths. Shortly before the accident, and at the place where the men died, apparently, one of their comrades had witnessed an angel surrounded by a white aura, hovering in the air.

In an effort to document and record the paranormal activity at the mansion and park, members of the snappily-titled Association for the Scientific Study of Anomalous Phenomenon spent several nights in the building in the early years of the twenty-first

The unfinished mansion, Woodchester Park.

century and were rewarded by several strange occurrences. A bell was heard ringing in an empty tower and the hands on a clock which had been stopped for repair were seen to have moved. These events seemed inexplicable, but more were to occur. The lights in the house suddenly illuminated the building once, even though there was no one present who could have switched them on. Long-haired women in the team felt their locks being tugged at by something unseen, and other team members became aware of a strange, persistent banging sound that seemed to approach them. As it became louder, the peculiar sound was recognised as the noise made by a steam engine at work. There is no railway line within a mile of the mansion.

In 2005 members of the Severnside Centre for Fortean Research conducted an overnight investigation at the mansion. Blue-coloured light phenomena manifested itself on the second-floor corridor – the first occurrence involved a perfect sphere of light, which rapidly travelled the corridor before disappearing at the knees of two of the investigators; in the second event the corridor was dimly illuminated for several seconds by a blue glow that descended from the rafters. CCTV footage recorded in the chapel of the mansion revealed what may have been the very vague form of a hooded figure, although this was far from conclusive.

The mansion has been studied by The Institute of Paranormal Research, too, and various examples of paranormal phenomena are said to have been experienced. These included the smell of candles in the disused chapel, stones being thrown through the air, and the sighting of several apparitions. Ghost walks, ghost hunts and paranormal investigations regularly take place at Woodchester, and it seems probable that the folklore – and perhaps the occasional bit of tangible evidence – surrounding the unfinished mansion place will only increase.

WOTTON-UNDER-EDGE

The town of Wotton-under-Edge sits at the most south-westerly tip of Gloucestershire, well on the way to Bristol. Although many might consider the town less attractive than some of its neighbours in the Cotswolds, it does have several curious features, the most interesting of these being an ancient dwelling in a road named Potters Pond. Thought to have been built in 1145, the house has very old timbers running through its walls and is called The Ram Inn – although it ceased trading as licensed premises in 1967 – and claims to be 'the most haunted house in Britain'.

All sorts of paranormal activities are supposed to have happened there. The owner has, apparently, been thrown across a room, pushed from behind on the stairs, and subjected to ghostly sex attacks. There are many old tales about bizarre and unsavoury goings-on at the former inn, including murders and unexplained deaths, devil worship and exorcisms. Lights have inexplicably flickered, people have felt the unpleasant sensation of cold hands upon their legs, once a puddle of water suddenly appeared on a wooden floor, and various apparitions are said to have been seen. These have included monks, witches, a Cavalier, a

The Ram Inn, Wooton-under-Edge.

tramp, a hanging man, a motorcyclist and, most often, a beautiful lady in a blue, hooded cape. The ghost of a shepherd haunts the first-floor area, and his dog has often been heard crossing the floor and scrabbling at a door in the former bar area. An 'evil' phantom black cat has been seen in the building, too, so perhaps the shepherd's dog was doing its best to get at it. One room in the old building is called 'The Bishop's Room' and this is where a young woman is supposed to have been strangled in the nineteenth century, after being kidnapped and robbed by a couple of highwaymen using the place as their base. A former Bishop of Gloucester, the Rt. Revd John Yates, visited the room some years ago, later stating that it was the most evil place he had ever had the misfortune to visit.

Given its reputation, it is not surprising that the place is regularly visited by 'ghost-busters' and sleuths hoping to find evidence of the paranormal. A team of investigators from The Ghost Club visited in 2003, and among the strange entities apparently encountered was an evil man in black and a distressed woman in her late teens named 'Anna'. In 2005 a television crew member claimed to have been attacked by a ghost in a barn at the property. It is difficult to know how seriously to take some of the accounts associated with Britain's 'most haunted house'. It is quite probable that some alleged experiences have been fuelled by expectation and imagination, but it seems unreasonable to dismiss all of the accounts in this way.

At least two of the town's current pubs are believed to be haunted. Various things have been moved around by an unseen hand at The Royal Oak – these activities being attributed to a ghost nicknamed 'George' – and The Falcon Inn has the ghost of an old lady who is said to live in the attic. Apparitions have been seen, too, of a little girl, a dog, and a man in his thirties.

Wotton's hostelries are not the only places in the town where ghosts are said to have been seen. The phantom of a woman with her hair on fire has apparently been seen – and heard – screaming as she runs along Symn Lane. According to tradition, she was murdered by her son in the nineteenth century. He had returned from Australia to claim his inheritance, was less than happy with the provision made for him, and killed her before setting light to her house. Whether he resigned himself to being caught is not known, but before his arrest he went up Wotton Hill to watch the house burn.

WYCK RISSINGTON

As far as is known, there have been no recent reports of incidences of haunting or other mysterious activities at Wyck Rissington. In the nave of the village church, however, there is a mosaic reproduction of a maze that used to be visible in the garden of the rectory. Opened to the public in 1953, the maze depicted 'the Mysteries of the Gospel' and was created by the village rector, Canon Harry Cheales, following a vivid dream.

Canon Cheales was particularly well known in the Cotswolds as an exorcist, and he visited numerous places in the area to investigate incidences of haunting and poltergeist activity. Considered an expert on the supernatural, he often spoke publicly to local groups and associations on his experiences, having begun dealing with ghosts and spirits when a poltergeist at his rectory ran up and down the stairs, rattled door handles and banged doors. Additionally, the ghost, which he called 'Geoffrey', had a pet cat, which would rub against one's legs and walk

The maze, Wyck Rissington Church.

145

through walls. Canon Cheales simply ordered the poltergeist to cease its troublesome activity, which it duly did.

He did not always consider it necessary to carry out an exorcism, and, where he believed a ghost to be completely harmless, he would, after praying, advise householders and witnesses that there was no cause for alarm. Canon Cheales retired in 1980 and the rectory was sold off and the maze cleared away. He died four years later, but he is still much remembered in the North Cotswolds as an exorcist one could call upon when troubled by persistent ghosts and poltergeists.

BIBLIOGRAPHY

Atkyns, Sir Robert, *The Ancient And Present State Of Gloucestershire* (1712)

Bagust, Harold, *A History Of Stow-On-The-Wold* (Aztec Publishing Co., 1979)

Belcher, Ernest Rambles, *Among The Cotswolds* (Privately Printed, 1892)

Briggs, Katharine, M. *The Folklore Of The Cotswolds* (Batsford, 1974)

Brooks, J.A., *Ghosts And Witches Of The Cotswolds* (Jarrold Publishing, 1981)

Bryant-Duncan, Dena, *True Ghost Stories Of The Forest Of Dean* (Manse Publications, 2009)

Clark, Leonard, *Who Killed The Bears?* (Forest of Dean Newspapers Limited, 1981)

Clarke, Stephen, *Ghosts Of Monmouth* (Monmouth Beacon, 1965)

Cope, Julian, *The Modern Antiquarian* (Thorsons, 1998)

Day, David, *All Over The Wold* (Seven Bowes-Lyon, 1998)

Dee, Joanna E., *Bibury* (Reardon Publishing, 1995)

Devereaux, Paul, *Ancient Earth Mysteries* (Cassell & Co, 2000)

Fennemore, E.P., *History Of Randwick* (Privately Printed, 1892)

Green, Andrew, *Ghosts of Today* (Kaye & Ward, 1980)

Hicks, Clive, *The Green Man: A Field Guide* (Compass Books, 2000)

Law, Sue, *Ghosts Of The Forest Of Dean* (Douglas Mclean, 1983)

Lee, Laurie, *Cider With Rosie* (The Hogarth Press, 1959)

Massingham, H.J., *Shepherd's Country* (Chapman & Hall 1938)

Matthews, Rupert, *Haunted Gloucestershire* (Logaston Press, 2006)

Palmer, Roy, *Folklore Of Gloucestershire* (Tempus, 2001)

Poulton-Smith, Anthony, *Paranormal Cotswolds* (Amberley, 2009)

Prosser, Carol, *Puzzle Wood* (Carol Prosser, 1984)

Somerville, Christopher, *Britain & Ireland's Best Wild Places* (Allen Lane 2008)

Sullivan, D.P., *Old Stones Of Gloucestershire* (Reardon & Son, 1991)

Sullivan, Danny, *Ley Lines* (Piatkus Books, 1999)

Turner, Mark, *Folklore & Mysteries Of The Cotswolds* (Hale, 1993)

Turner, Mark, *Curious Cotswolds* (Tempus, 2006)

Turner, Mark, *Inns & Pubs of The Cotswolds* (Tempus, 2007)

Walker, Charles, *Strange Britain* (Brian Trodd Publishing, 1989)

Watkins, Alfred, *The Old Straight Track* (Methuen, 1925)

Westwood, Jennifer & Simpson, Jacqueline, *The Penguin Book Of Ghosts* (Allen Lane, 2008)

Whittington-Egan, Richard, *The Great British Torso Mystery* (The Bluecoat Press, 2002)

NEWSPAPERS & JOURNALS

Cheltenham Chronicle and Gloucestershire Graphic
The Citizen
Cotswold Journal
The Daily Telegraph
Gloucestershire Echo
Wiltshire and Gloucestershire Standard
The Forester
The Independent

WEBSITES

www.bbc.co.uk/gloucestershire
www.darkstar1.co.uk/GlosUFOs
www.grahamthomas.com/history5
www.jharding.demon.co.uk/SheelaNaGigIndex
http://parafort.com/strangestroud
www.taynton.btinternet.co.uk/fleur
www.twistedtree.org.uk
www.ufoinfo.com/sightings/uk
www.ufos-aliens.co.uk

LOCATIONS BY DISTRICT

It will be seen that all of the towns and villages included in this book are described in a simple A–Z gazetteer format. For those wishing to examine entries by reference to geographical area, however, locations within particular districts can be identified as follows:

NORTH COTSWOLDS

Aston Magna
Blockley
Bourton-on-the-Hill
Bourton-on-the-Water
Broad Campden
Broadwell
Chipping Campden
Compton Abdale
Draycott
Ebrington
Evenlode
Great Barrington
Great Rissington
Guiting Power
Hailes
Hampnett
Longborough
Lower Swell
Maugersbury
Mickleton
Moreton-in-Marsh
Naunton
Northleach
Saintbury
Sherborne
Shipton Oliffe
Snowshill
Stanton
Stanway
Stow-on-the-Wold
Todenham
Withington
Wyck Rissington

CHELTENHAM, CIRENCESTER AND TEWKESBURY

Aldsworth
Ampney Crucis
Ampney St Peter
Bagendon
Baunton
Bibury
Bishop's Cleeve
Cerney Wick
Chedworth
Cheltenham
Cirencester
Coombe Hill
Deerhurst
Dumbleton
Duntisbourne Abbots
Elkstone
Fairford
Kempsford
Lechlade
Little Washbourne
North Cerney
Painswick
Poulton
Prestbury
Sheepscombe
South Cerney
Tewkesbury
Tirley
Tredington
Winchcombe

STROUD VALLEY

Amberley
Avening
Bisley
Chalford
Charfield
Cherington
Coaley
Dursley
Edge
France Lynch
Frocester
Hyde
Kingswood
Leonard Stanley
Minchinhampton
Nailsworth
North Nibley
Owlpen
Ozleworth
Randwick
Rodborough
Selsley
Slad
Sling
Stroud
Tetbury
Thrupp
Woodchester
Wotton-under-Edge

GLOUCESTER AND THE FOREST OF DEAN

Arlingham
Berkeley
Birdlip
Clearwell
Coleford
Cranham
Dymock
Flaxley
Frampton-on-Severn
Gloucester
Hardwicke
Littledean
Longney
Lydbrook
Lydney
May Hill
Newent
Newland
Parkend
Redbrook
Redmarley D'Abitot
Ruardean
Ruspidge
St Briavels
Saul
Soudley
Staunton
Upton St Leonards
Westbury-on-Severn

INDEX

Other titles published by The History Press

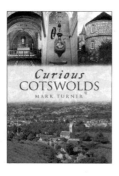

Curious Cotswolds
MARK TURNER

Curious Cotswolds takes the reader on a tour of the area, looking at the history, archaeology and curiosities of the Cotswolds. The author, a former Cotswolds policeman, describes points of interest to be found in the towns, villages and hamlets of the region, looking at Cheltenham and North; Cirencester, Stroud and South; Worcestershire and Warwickshire; and Oxfordshire. This historical guide offers a fascinating insight into the Cotswolds and will delight visitors and residents alike.

978 0 7524 3930 3

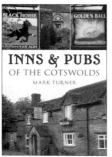

Inns & Pubs of the Cotswolds
MARK TURNER

This A–Z covering Gloucestershire, Oxfordshire, Warwickshire and Worcestershire is a delightful tour around the most interesting pubs in the area. Taking in all manner of establishments such as the Coach and Horses, in Longborough, to the White Hart Royal Hotel, a sixteenth-century inn in Moreton-on-Marsh, the author visits a huge variety of pubs that have made the Cotswolds the delightful area they are today. It is sure to appeal to those who live in the Cotswolds and visitors wishing to tour the area's charming pubs.

978 0 7524 4465 9

Ghost Hunting: A Survivor's Guide
JOHN FRASER

The Roman scholar Pliny the Younger was one of the first to write about ghost hunting. Two thousand years later, and the hunt still goes on. For all the thousands of hours spent by investigators in cold, dark houses, ghosts remain elusive and unproven. This book sets out to be a practical guide to ghost hunting. Examining cases from the past and the present day, this book asks if it is possible to find the truth in this age-old quest.

978 0 7524 5414 6

The Little Book of the Paranormal
RUPERT MATTHEWS

The paranormal is a subject of endless fascination to mankind. There is an insatiable appetite for tales of UFOs, ghosts, cryptozoology and other features of our world that are frequently reported by eye-witnesses. This little book introduces the reader to the world of the paranormal and entertains them with numerous anecdotes, snippets of information and lists of events. Rupert Matthews has produced an amusing, and yet serious volume that will leave the reader wondering over the amazing world of the paranormal.

978 0 7524 5165 7

Visit our website and discover thousands of other History Press books.

www.thehistorypress.co.uk